# SPIRITUAL WEALTH
# MANAGEMENT

The Abundance Bible & Prosperity Manifesto

George S Mentz JD MBA CWM

BALBOA.
PRESS
A DIVISION OF HAY HOUSE

Balboa Press books may be ordered through booksellers or by contacting:

Balboa Press
A Division of Hay House
1663 Liberty Drive
Bloomington, IN 47403
www.balboapress.com
1-(877) 407-4847

ISBN: 978-1-4525-5741-0 (sc)
ISBN: 978-1-4525-5743-4 (hc)
ISBN: 978-1-4525-5742-7 (e)

Library of Congress Control Number: 2012915228

Printed in the United States of America

Balboa Press rev. date: 07/08/2013

# CONTENTS

# INTRODUCTION TO WEALTH

This book is for those who desire wealth and prosperity. The wisdom herein is for seekers who are open to new perspectives and who want to live to the fullest. This manuscript is designed to help readers make a difference in the world by helping people make the best of themselves and their opportunities. For those of you who want more out of life, and who are tired of failure, this collection of timeless success wisdom will show you the path to achievement and the keys to prosperity. Do not sit idly by and reject or deny the abundance of the world—abundance awaits your cooperation and inquiry. The world is plentiful with resources, and your creativity is one of the many secrets to your future success. You do not need money to plan and to begin working on an idea; you do not need a special talent or to save every penny to be rich. You do not need the perfect business location for your offices. Many people become rich with no talent, no college education, a less than perfect place to work and live, and no start-up capital. The time is now to change your mind about life and to begin anew. When you are ready and willing to improve your life and to open your heart and mind, the gold mine of abundance will be available to you. The whole world of past and present is looking toward you, waiting for you to achieve your dreams; all you need to do is make the mental and spiritual shift in consciousness.

Much of this book is about tapping into the energy of the universe. I call it spiritual or cosmic energy, or God force or power. There are many words that have been used over the centuries to describe the Source and obtaining flow and unity with universal power—God, Spirit, the Good, Universal Mind,

Deity, Lord, Infinite, Almighty, Creator, and Universal Life Force. In this book, I will focus on Abundance, or the everlasting creative forces or powers that are available to anyone who wants to be an architect of good and constructive things in order to better one's own life and the lives of those one cares about in this world.

# WEALTH PHILOSOPHY

As we mature in life, all of us develop an internal hunger for a higher purpose and to master our destiny. This innate fire in the belly seemingly compels us to think and take action; we must change and adapt. Growth is necessary for the human condition. Finding a reason for being, where we can cultivate our talents and use them to improve life for ourselves and those we love, becomes vitally important. Striving for the personal best in ourselves while serving humanity is an ideal both important and noble. It is part of our desire for a greater good. Becoming the best we can be and doing the things we love to do in service and in leisure is a natural desire. This is true whether one is a fan of Sun-Tzu, John Stuart Mill, Buddhism, or Shakespeare. The state of Abundance is possible when we inherently understand the need to adapt, grow, and be prepared. You hold the golden key when you master your destiny by improving yourself in mind body and spirit.

This codex is a summary of the key philosophy and secrets needed to advance to your highest potential. If you need to learn even more to prepare yourself for this guide, we suggest several other authors: Marcus Aurelius, the gospels of Jesus Christ, Buddha, Pythagoras, Hegel, Kant, Emerson, von Goethe, Meister Eckhart, poetic Vedas and Eddas, the Book of Psalms, Zoroaster, Lao Tzu, Socrates, Plato, Aristotle, the Upanishads, and any great wisdom literature. Then, of course, we can seek more light from the authors in the bibliography.

One of the greatest secrets of mankind is that leaders and professionals have quietly used the philosophy contained herein for centuries. Keep this book close, use this secret technology, and master your destiny.

Whatever our vocation may be (e.g., mechanic or artist), you will need the right instruction and tools to gain excellence. The importance of natural expression is absolutely necessary for personal accomplishment and prosperity. Your highest form of expression requires an imaginative and resourceful life; it involves the abundance of ideas, things, and actions.

True and lasting prosperity has a spiritual foundation and balance. Genuine success is mastering excellence in body, mind, and spirit. When there is balance, ideas and energy naturally come from the universe to the person who is exercising this higher order of existence. When we are at our best and acting as effective individuals, we actually have more insights flowing to us from the universal source or consciousness of the infinite.

Rene Descartes simplifies the essence of this philosophy: "I think, therefore I am." With this statement, we must be able to find our being, or what people call their is-ness. The key is to reconnect your spirit and being-ness with the universe in a way that is harmonious.

George W. F. Hegel, a German philosopher, also believed that reality was absolute Spirit; we participate in our destinies and create our own realities. The iconic spiritual minds of the Renaissance professed that it is the right of the individual to have a direct experience with a deity through prayer, meditation, and a return to the spiritual core. Meister Eckhart, the fourteenth-century Christian Neo-Platonist, personified the spiritual basics in these words: "If the only prayer you say in your life is 'Thank You,' that would suffice."

To maintain effective growth, one must have a mental and spiritual tune-up that involves a complete cathartic mental inventory and assessment. Elimination of destructive beliefs is necessary. Find out and write out what you don't want in your life anymore; decide to discard the mental rubbish. Learn from your mistakes and begin anew.

Ancient Greeks such as Socrates said, "Know thyself," and, "The unexamined life is not worth living." Be willing to take a hard look at yourself in the mirror, and seek an honest appraisal of your character and behavior.

The French existentialist Jean-Paul Sartre was clear about accountability. We should start having responsibility for our actions going forward and refuse to be bogged down with self-victimization and blaming others. Put the past behind you.

Begin a mental examination and compile a written list of what you do want from life. Examine this list every day for thirty days, adding and subtracting from it as needed. Identify causes and reasons for success and failure, and try to eliminate the habits associated with failure. Take an honest look at your track record over the years. Become ready to change and advance, stepping toward a revitalized and better life.

While working on your list, be willing to forgive yourself and others. If you must, pray for forgiveness toward or from others every day for thirty days. Pray for yourself, and pray for people you love, those you hate, the poor, the rich, and the successful. Pray for health. Most important, pray and express thanks that you have the ability to change and grow. Ben Franklin, in his autobiography, used a process called the precept of order, where each day he took time to review his day, set goals, and see where he could improve his actions and character.

Learning forgiveness and non-attachment is a key strategy to free up the heart, mind, and soul. Think about the word Revelation or (reveal-ation) or the art of diagnosing or discussing past problems. This action clears your spiritual mind, freeing it to receive divine ideas. Become willing to atone, forgive, and clear your mind to a state of true openness. Face the part of your mind's eye that holds you back. When Nietzsche said, "That which does not kill us makes us stronger," he probably meant that we need to face fear and get out of our comfort zones.

You *must* let go of those beliefs of limitation. There is *no* limit on love, on ideas, on gratitude, and on you developing a consciousness of abundance, health, and love. Focus your heart and mind on prosperity and contemplate the blessings that you have already received.

The universe is limitless, and you have the ability to think ideas that can become the form of your character and future. As Marcus Aurelius so eloquently said, "Take full account of the excellencies which you possess, and in gratitude remember how you would hanker after them, if you had them not." The reign of Aurelius was part of an era known as the era of five good emperors. History has acclaimed him for his philosophical writings titled *Meditations*. Aurelius includes another great quote that we should follow: "It is not death that a man should fear, but he should fear never beginning to live."

If you consider the insights of humanistic psychologists such as Carl Rogers and Abraham Maslow, it is said that people have an innate drive to be all they can be and to self-actualize. This intrinsic metaphysics plays a large role in facilitating the progression of the best in each of us.

### Desire: What Do You Really Want in Life?

What are your burning desires? What do you really want most in your life? What do you want in earnest? What would make you feel alive and like a child, as if you are on your true path? Contemplate Aristotle's theory of potentiality: "Within each of us is a natural evolution toward fulfilling our potential."

Make a list of your past successes. Making a list of what is good in your life and what you are feeling grateful for will energize your soul with constructive belief and appreciation. As Immanuel Kant has implied that Perception is our reality. These are the matters that help construct how you perceive life events and what gives them meaning and importance to you. If you focus your thoughts on the best, then you will attract the best. Feed yourself with things that are good, learning about what is excellent, and these things will build your worldview and character.

Tap into the universe for insights regarding your new ideas and goals. Make up your mind to cooperate with the Supreme Force by being thankful for all you have; appreciate life, praise others, and engage gratitude. Allow yourself to love the inherent goodness of the world. This mental attunement and earnest thankfulness will activate the connecting link that is inside of you. Next, begin to daily imagine yourself in your mind's eye as totally happy, healthy, and successful. Visualize yourself in your sacred and peaceful place with your spiritual double (the image and person who you see as you in your mind). Commune with your sacred self about what you should do to grow, improve, and expand your life.

## Visualize Positive Outcomes

When visualizing the outcome of your chosen path or goal, allow yourself to feel joy, relaxation, acceptance, truth, and peaceful victory in relation to your positive visualization. Make all of your thought forms constructive, think of becoming who you want to be, and imagine how your objectives will benefit all involved; then contemplate the essence of your goals. The essence is the reason that the vision is good and righteous. As such, the *essence* is where you understand the how and why of your wants, and decide how you will use the good that comes to you when it arrives.

Concentrate on what you want to become; finding your higher purposes and direction should become your spiritual goal. With that being said, get in touch with your natural inclinations. The legendary Dr. Carl Jung theorized that one finds their natural talents deep within the spirit of one's self. When we get in touch with our natural inclinations, it elevates our outward expression. It may not be easy, but if you act toward your higher purpose each day, the cosmic momentum will build to your advantage. The daily completion of purposeful and constructive thinking allows for creation to add increase into your life.

After your desire and mental image is pictured as best as you can in your mind's eye, you should send, let go of, and surrender your vision as a letter or petition to the abundant universe. After sending the vision out from your mind and heart, always mentally permit the highest outcome to manifest, and be willing to receive the best result.

In moments of doubtful circumstance, practice gratitude and count your blessings. Affirmations and decrees strengthen your vision and conviction. An affirmation or decree can be a prayer or meditation that asserts our prosperous, happy, and successful bounty. Many people simply say aloud, "I am whole, abundant, complete, healthy, happy, and successful." That is just one example, but you can make up your own positive affirmations. You need not use the words "not" or "no." Affirm by saying, "I am blessed," or "I am happy," or "I am rich in love and life." Whether or not it is your reality at this moment, it should not stand in your way—say it and believe it. Feel it as if it were true right now. The attitude of health, wealth, and peace of mind is a priceless asset that even the richest people on earth cherish.

Stake your claim on developing a consciousness of plenty. Begin to believe that you are now a co-creator and not just at the whim of the world. See your future with an attitude of liberation, faith, knowingness, cheer, and earnestness. The cards of life will begin to be stacked in your favor, and you will know it.

When you are determined to master a consciousness of prosperity and creativity, you must also give with an open heart. Donations of service, time, and money to others or organizations that are divinely inspiring can create a space or vacuum, which magnetically draws more good to you. Further, when we give from the heart without expectation of return, the plentiful universe showers us with opportunity.

The beauty of your spirit is individualized but is also connected to the Infinite. Both Aristotle and Thomas Aquinas refer to God as the 'First Cause" or "Pure Mind." In essence, we come from this pure mind and first cause; we are created from the Source. We have desires and ideas flowing to us from a higher source at all times. What you do with your ideas and imagination is of extreme importance. Your ideas are yours, they are priceless, and they are consciously coming to you in every moment. Your creativity is your abundance. Express you earnest desires to your deeper self and spirit; listen to your heart and listen to your soul. Some call it intuition, and others call it a sixth sense. When you are operating at a higher level of spiritual consciousness, you will see, feel, and comprehend important ideas, and it is your job to take action on the insights that are best for your higher purpose.

## Action: Start Things and Finish Them

Next is action. Remember, action is what separates the men from the boys. Do at least three things each day toward your higher purpose. Do your research and learn what you need to know to accomplish your goals, but in the meantime, take steps to start things and finish them. The poet Johann Wolfgang von Goethe famously stated that "boldness is genius." Acclaimed author Robert Collier also believed that beginning any task created a nucleus of activity, bringing form from the formless. If you begin something and maintain faith in the process, you may then utilize the act of gratitude and praise which is like watering a flower with nourishment. In the same way a flower needs water, the universe craves peace, thanks, praise, and action, and the universe will respond accordingly with blessings. Develop a harmonious spiritual relationship with the universe and you will see results. As with the stoics and

Emperor Marcus Aurelius, if you have tried to do your best in this world, then that is all you can do; doing and being your best is its own reward. The stoics had a healthy sense of apathy and moderation, and they did not allow the challenges of life to stop their focused work and righteous living.

There are many facets to productivity, but you must know that if you have your spiritual, physical, and mental health operating at a higher level, your productivity, flow, and the fruits of your labor will be much greater for yourself and all involved. Even the early socialist or communist thinkers such as Engels and Marx believed firmly in productivity as the key to progress.

The big metaphysical secret lies in becoming one with your desires, because you then become in tune with your objective! When we blend purpose and spirituality, our energy then becomes laser focused.

It is no wonder that the subject of mental concentration was such a hot topic a hundred years ago. Relative to the topic of concentration were discussions about focus, burning desire, and never looking back. This type of mindful action and persistence becomes the moral fiber to any success. Partner this targeted drive to a creative plan, and it becomes the catalyst to expand our world.

When you are acting with elevated character and confidence, you will sense a new found self-respect. Higher-quality relationships are inevitable when you are building your confidence, poise, enthusiasm, and being purpose driven. As for your speech and thinking, constructive talk is important; avoid toxic thoughts. The philosopher of existentialism Soren Kierkegaard was famous for saying, "We must think for ourselves and be suspicious of groupthink, and we should not worry about the ignorance of neighbors and society."

## Surround Yourself with Experts

To keep your state of mind focused, avoid thoughts of deficiency and hardship. The birds of the sky and the lilies of the field are fed and clothed by the abundant universe. In the same way, you should only speak of constructive issues, praise others, and become a ray of sunshine to yourself and your community. Remember, sunlight is God's disinfectant.

When you become determined to expect the best in life, you will make a dynamic shift in thinking where you are waking up on the proverbial right side of the bed almost every day. You will begin to believe that complaining and blaming are a waste of your time; your time is now specifically used as a constructive force for advancement. Some people expect the good, while others expect the bad. Remember, Emerson, St. Augustine, and Plato believed that evil is not a diabolical force but rather the absence of good. Overall, self suffering is not a prerequisite for peace of mind.

Love, gratitude, and enthusiasm are very powerful forces for your betterment. Your love energy is a form of charisma and attraction power. Learning to experience love, joy, and enthusiasm may take some practice, but once you begin to feel it, it will be as a force that precedes you like an aura and can be transmuted into tangible energy, which allows you to do great things.

As you become a powerful, creative, and attractive person, your energies can be used for righteous living and working in a labor of love, which will be like play. Henry David Thoreau believed that we should put our "Conscience before conformity." Thus, your natural creativity and labor will be fun, and you will actually learn to freely accept premium can and rewards for your quality services and the products in relation to your craft.

British political philosopher John Locke believed in a liberal, anti-authoritarian theory of the state. His practical theory of knowledge advocated religious toleration and personal identity. His philosophy suggests that order is necessary to protect the individual, and man is endowed with inalienable rights where these rights are gained through work and effort.

Be conscious of your fullness of the good things such as life, health, love, and the ability to be in spiritual unity with the deity of your choosing. Become in love with your higher spiritual power. Develop the consciousness of prosperity and open your mind to being worthy of receiving of all of the good the universe has to offer. Be ready, willing, and prepared to receive good.

The results of practicing these principles and suggestions will result in a natural expression of your life purpose that becomes a reality—you will become who you were meant to be. It may require great energy from you, but it will feel eventually like child's play. You may find many challenges, but the experience of life will be invigorating when you pause in those moments to stop and smell the roses. Life is delicate and sometimes short, and you may be compelled to dedicate energy to definitive ends. All mortals are faced with these timeless questions: What do you want to be remembered for? How do you want to impact the world? What is your potential legacy?

The nineteenth-century European philosopher Arthur Schopenhauer believed that thinking of things of aesthetic appreciation temporarily allows us a respite from the strife of desire, and it also allows us to enter a realm of purely mental enjoyment. Schopenhauer's writings contend that we are motivated by our will, and it is our will that is our sense of reality. Therefore, willingness is at the core of our growth and advancement. Desire is good and comes from the Spirit. Seeing past the illusion of what seems apparent, and acting on healthy desires, is the key to growth and happiness.

Whether you are a student of Locke, Emerson, Ayn Rand, Ben Franklin, Frederick Douglas, or Buddha, there are some eternal truths. The great lesson from many of the world's legendary philosophers is that the individual is an important and unique part of the whole. Each person should master themselves; education, knowledge, and inner peace are essential. Efficient effort is vital for advancement. Growing in faith, knowingness, and wisdom are all important factors of duty to ourselves and to society. Your contributions may seem small, but your spiritual creativity and service may positively affect generations to come. Overall, the ripple effect of one pebble tossed in the lake has a broad impact on the whole of its contents.

From Taoism to Christianity, and from Eastern and Western cultures, the mystics believed in a timeless and formless force that governs the cosmos. Most of the founding fathers of the United States were deists who believed in the Source or a supreme God. We are born of this cosmic force, and we have the ability to more effectively cooperate as spiritual and physical beings in conjunction with this force. Listen to your heart and allow yourself to become and evolve into your highest expression; get in tune with the world and begin to master your destiny.

In the following chapters we will do three things.
- ✓ **Examine** some of the greatest spiritual laws known to mankind
- ✓ **Read** about and **experience** some exercises.
- ✓ **Learn** new and effective success and wealth strategies.

## *You Are Chosen, Naturally Unique, Knowing.*

---

It does not matter from what ancestry you have come—you *must* believe that it is good and great. Whatever your education, believe that you can be better as you gain more knowledge and understanding of the laws of life. Regardless of your appearances, you can improve yourself, be healthy, and enhance your image in your own unique way. It does not matter what religion or philosophy you adhere to; your spiritual knowledge and awareness can be cultivated to a new dimension where peace of mind and abundance is yours.

You hold potential greatness, and it awaits you. You have been chosen to do great things and live a significant life. You have great talents from the universe, and it is a gift that must be nourished.

Only good can come from growth. Sometimes change is difficult, but the reinvention or rebirth of your true purpose is available now.[1]

You must allow your assets and skills to be honed and sharpened—do not die with your vision and talents unused. You are special, and you can be whatever you want within your reach and grow toward your true destiny.

# PART I:

# THE METAPHYSICAL SECRETS

## *How the Mind Creates Your World—*
## *The Path to Abundance*

### You Have a Birthright to Wealth and Prosperity

The definition of abundance and true wealth is arguably the free and unrestricted use of all the things that may be necessary for you to advance in the direction of your dreams and potential, thus attaining your fullest mental, spiritual, and physical prosperity. You have a right to wealth. Wealth is that basic desire to have a richer, fuller, and more abundant life. We all should live for the equal advancement and fulfillment of body, mind, and soul; there is no reason we should limit our capacities in any of the three sectors.

Many associate greed, lust, and arrogance as a constituent of the rich, and they wonder if wealthy people are truly happy. Ironically, it is poverty which disheartens the spirit in human relationships, including those we love. Poverty undermines self-esteem, confidence, and our outlook upon life. With poverty as a state of mind and life, we are empty to give to those whom we love and care about. Poverty limits our ability to connect to people and the world. Poverty incapacitates giving, which is the demonstration of love and compassion.

1

Abundance and creation are forms of wealth, and therefore we must get in tune with creativity. When we do, prosperity will appear in our lives.

Creativity, innovation, and abundance will go to the people who flow and cooperate with life and not reject it. Nature has an inexhaustible source of riches. Accordingly, it is natural to seek more from life, and your advancement is vital for your growth. As the saying goes, we grow or die. With a higher plane and dimension, we can now make forty years' worth of advancement in three to six years, with efficiency.

As an example, the last one hundred years of science have shown more life-giving and technological improvements than the last two thousand years. This is proof that rapid advancement is available with freedom and discipline at your command.

We will now show you the first secret of life. This key to success can be yours if you simply accept the following statement. Just take it as fact, and the world will begin to move with you.

## *Thoughts and Wealth Creation*

How we construct our thoughts and emotions assists in the manifestation of physical forms and our character. Our worldview is also malleable and can be a great catalyst to creation. Positive and negative thinking facilitates constructive or deconstructive results. For instance, the statement "I need more money" lends the subject to continual detrimental thoughts to "need more money." Changing the focus to a goal (having more money) rather than the problem (needing more money) results in a positive perspective. Rephrasing this thought in a positive manner would be, "I will find opportunity that yields greater and greater rewards."

If you conceive of your desire, you can then imagine that your goal will take place with belief, and then, you will be able retrieve the opportunity from the world's storehouse of riches. As a rule, man originates thought; thought turns into plans or mental images in the mind. Man can communicate his thought and mental images into and throughout the world. This creation begins with our thoughts focused within and without. Your mind is the center of your world. Your thoughts, mixed with a thankful heart directed toward your goals, can flow out into the world as creative energy. You mentally picture and believe that your healthy goal is possible. Understand the essence and reasons that you should have this type of result in your life; you envision your desired outcome with specificity. You think of and picture the opportunity frequently, and you believe that you have the type of result that you desire, feeling it and harvesting the emotion of having it as much as possible.

These thoughts and a mental practice of visualization will be sent off into the world like a letter of request. If you practice this visualization enough, the desires you have will be met. Truth is your faithful, non-doubting interpretation of your thoughts. Do not focus on failure, poverty, disease, or deficiencies—your truth is health, riches, success, and happiness. Do not doubt or speak against your thoughts and dreams. Keep these mental petitions as faithful as possible while living harmoniously with people, places, institutions, and the universe.

It is the desire of the Source that you should have all that you need. You will begin with a simple desire for some type of improvement in life; a desire coupled with unwavering faith will correctly unfold for you over time. The motives of your desires are important: you want to help yourself and others, and you do not want to cause harm in the process.

You will achieve these desires much more quickly if your motives are not colored with greed, ego, pride, lust, competition, hate, resentment, and arrogance. Your desires must be propelled by love, gratitude, faith, confidence, mental focus, truth, acceptance, creativity, positive expectation, and clear planning, and you should give more love and value than you take.

## Desire and Purpose

Desire is the motivating force that rules the world. Even with today's attitudes—where science, philosophy, and religious metaphysics cross paths—most have acknowledged that: finding purpose, natural expression, mission, and one's true place are all major factors in self-expression and spirit-manifestation. Where a person's true purpose is frustrated, reactions take place, and most people are guided and again redirected by their burning desires toward their highest ideal of creativity and function.

## To Begin Your Process of Prosperity

Brainstorm on your ideas each day, clarifying in your mind exactly what you want and how you will achieve it. Hold the picture of the moment you have completed the achievement with positive certainty; never speak or think of it as not being possible, and claim the picture of success as a fact and that it is already yours in mind. Keep your mind tuned in to the universal presence and energy by having a thankful heart and grateful thoughts. If you cannot be grateful, then begin to think of your ability to walk, talk, see, hear, travel, and speak. These are the simplest of freedoms to be grateful for, and they are easily overlooked. Good health is one of these simple freedoms we should recognize with gratitude; in doing so, it initiates a powerful, positive outlook. This new perspective connects you to life and your dreams. People will soon sense this new outlook and serenity that you are projecting.

Remember that you must exercise this mental picturing and thankfulness every day for at least a month. However, after a month, you will not believe the difference in your perception of life. Do not be frightened or ashamed to ask for what you really want. Ask for more than you need. The world is full of people to give and receive. Never be frightened to receive—receive with humility, thankfulness, and appreciation. In the final analysis, extreme poverty and self-sacrifice are not pleasing to anyone, and extreme altruism is just as dangerous as extreme greed. Thus, give and receive with joy.

There is a creative universal force from which unlimited abundance flows. It will give us all that we need and desire when we have a pure heart. A pure heart and mind simply means that you do not allow the weeds of ignorance, bitterness, hate, and irritation to cloud and fill your mind. To facilitate a mind of purity, make the profound connection to the universal spirit within by developing a strong feeling of thankfulness for life, love, health, and material gifts that you already have or will have.

Let us think about gratitude and thankfulness. Can you have happiness with a bitter heart? Can you have real faith when you are constantly blaming, angry, and ungrateful? If you think you can be happy with a blaming, hateful, and bitter mind, then good luck. If you want to change to an outlook on life where you feel that all is possible, then keep reading.

Think back and reflect on the times in your life when you got what you wanted and became arrogant or egotistical. After you received some good fortune, you forgot your humility and abandoned your connection to your universal Spirit. You may have given up your relationship with spirituality because you thought you had won the game of life.

In times of good fortune, it is especially important to exercise and practice grateful thoughts. Doing so continues the flow of riches to us and expands your focus. What becomes important to you will come to you and remain with you. If you have doubt and fear, you will disperse fear and doubt. Gratitude will keep you connected to the world and afford you a harmonious relationship with all, because gratitude and thankfulness prevent dissatisfaction. Continue to fix your attention in appreciation for the best in life; fix your mind on health, love, success, and good fortune. Your faith will be renewed and strengthened from your own consciousness of gratitude.

## Energize Gratitude

There are many ways to promote greater peace of mind. Generally, there is no better method to increase a sense of tranquility than to cultivate a mindset of thankfulness. A good mental practice is to add a five-minute gratitude exercise to your daily routine. Think about or write out a list of things for which to be grateful for today. This exercise will brings wondrous results. You may not feel results overnight, but within a month you will feel and see the change toward a positive perspective, which becomes a greater worldview. In addition to gratitude, exercise a ban on negativity for one week. Complaining attracts destructive people, places, and things into your life. Each time you find yourself complaining, touch each of your shoulders with your finger and proclaim, "I am abundance."

If you have trouble with certain negative triggers, then eliminate them. If politics bothers you, then quit reading the paper for a short while. If certain people constantly annoy you, then you should avoid them for a time, too. You are working on yourself, and it is okay to take care of your well-being first. The people around you will be happy in the end, if you rebuild and renew your positive spirit and enthusiasm for life as a priority. This is putting your health first, in this case your spiritual health.

## Success Agreement

Your desires should be very specific, and your mental blueprint must be just as precise. For example, you may write out on a piece of paper a personal agreement with yourself:

> *I, Jane Doe, will have a successful business and I will live in a beautiful three-thousand-square-foot home in the Tudor style near Central Park. I am the best I can be in my job and company, and I am very successful in my position, selling creative products and services. I give the highest quality service and value to my clients. My products and services will have outstanding benefits and will help all of my customers. I do all of these things, work hard, and be persistent in my purpose and labor. I will not give up. People will be glad to pay me for my services because they are a benefit to all. I gladly accept compensation and do what I need to do to receive the payment. I will use the fruits of my creativity to build my business, invest in myself, enjoy life, help those I love, follow my dreams, and live in the home of my dreams.*

## Send Your Petition to the World like a Request That Must Be Granted

Spend each day contemplating your personal commitment. Visualize the success and form an attractive mental image— moving into your beautiful home, helping those you love, or a bonus check for great work. Mentally imagine yourself in that very moment of completing the transaction with joy. Feel it, gather the emotion, and believe that an outcome (or an even better one) is possible. Moreover, you should know, feel, and see in your mind what you will do when you have the wonderful home or outstanding wealth. Then think how you will live, help others, and serve humanity.

A clearer picture strengthens our desire. If your desire is strong, your willingness to focus on the success and to claim it as yours will become a seamless transaction. Each day you must engage your heartfelt faith to secure small steps toward success. Stay engaged in moving ahead with your goals amid gratitude and faith. After you picture your optimal vision and read your personal agreement to yourself, complete the meditative thought process with words of gratitude: "Thank you for the blessing," "Thank you for expanding the quality of my life," and "Thank you for protecting me and my family." This will complete your exercise. Send this petition into the world like a request that must be granted. Then, you should be ready to receive what you want in any form, or even a higher result.

As for willpower, you need only cultivate the idea of willingness upon yourself. Your self-will should be used to think about precise constructive plans and doing specific beneficial actions. Every moment spent in uncertainty is a waste of time—direct your attention to prosperity. The best thing you can do for the non-believers is to show them that you can achieve abundance and success. Your efforts will be a success if your actions are based in a strong desire where you are willing to go the distance to fulfill it.

Do not tell the same doubtful people of your dreams and ideas. If you tell enough bitter people about your idea, their collective doubt or jealousy may weaken and sabotage your energy. Surround yourself with successful people, experts in the field, and people who are encouraging and insightful and working toward a new outlook on life.

## Always See the Positive Side of
## Your Present State of Affairs

Interest yourself in becoming rich in life, and always try to see the positive side of your present state of affairs. Focus on optimistic conversation or beneficial events that have happened in your life. Make lists of things to do and begin doing them one by one. It may take a year to complete, but you must begin somewhere. Do each series of tasks and individual actions efficiently. Don't worry about the past or the future or incessantly moan to others about your difficulties or failures. Focus on prosperity today.

## Do Only What Can Be Done Today;
## Tomorrow We Can Begin Anew

Take action today. Write our plans for your future for this year, the next 3 years, and even 5 or 10 years in the future. Begin to do tasks each day to improve your lot in life and help others. Do your tasks correctly the first time, and you need not fix them later. To do efficient and effective work, you need only to do one thing at a time and to not spread yourself too thin. Focus on the now and make your plans incremental or step-driven. One step at a time, with focus and effectiveness, will virtually guarantee success.

You need not try and mandate an outcome. The creative forces will unfold the correct and highest result for you; you merely need to aim in the direction of your dreams with focus and organize your affairs, so that you are prepared to receive the success and gladly accept the payoff. Overall, action is what will allow you to receive your abundance. Do only what can be done today, and tomorrow you can begin anew. In sum, put the faith, vision, and purpose behind your every action to accelerate the path to your higher abundance.

# *Discover Your Purpose!*

## Write a List of Twenty Things of Interest to You

You should determine what you like and what you love to do through this simple process. Write a list of twenty things of interest to you; continue adding and subtracting from the list. Over time, you will development meaningful ideas because your higher consciousness will guide you toward your given talents. As a note, your purpose could be to research history or science, to read books, to write articles or books, to develop written content, to draw or create art and graphics, to travel, or to communicate with people. Over time your definite purpose should become more specific, such as "I intend to become the best speaker or writer on the topic of politics or taxes, complete a masters or doctorate in international business, and build the best website for information and links to success literature." It does not matter how you start, just begin the writing process! Remember that a good talent (something you like to do and you are good at doing) combined with desire to become the best in a given field of work will ensure that you will do what you love. At the least, you can become a trainer of your trade or profession and give back to the world by accelerating the learning of children or students in your field.

Without being boastful, you must convey the impression to others that you are an exemplarily human being for all who come in contact with you. Impress on others that you can add to their lives; speak of your life and business as getting better and better all of the time. Act and feel as though you are successful, as if you are already rich in life and all your needs are met. Incorporate a compassionate humility that you blend with poise, faith, confidence, and self-esteem. You need only speak when necessary, but your strong character and faithful confidence will attract the best people into your life.

## Use Your Present Job Skillfully to Move in the Direction That You Want

If you are in a job and cannot leave it to immediately follow your dreams, then do what you can in the evenings or weekends to hone your skills, plans, and education toward your goal. Use your existing position to move in the direction that you want. There are thousands of people who have their business pay for their part-time education; your contacts at work may even lead to a better or different job. In business, you must also be prepared to discuss your dreams (what you want from life) in spoken words. You should know exactly what you want, and you should be able to clarify and quantify your ideas to others in an enthusiastic way. Be able to ask for and accept what you want out of life. You will need to interact with others who can help you. This process of abundance, harmonization, and advancement will lead others to want to help you. Be ready for them, and be open to forming alliances with others. Thus, your visions, meditations, and requests are traditionally answered by the universal power in the form of other people or entities being available to help and guide you—be ready to tell them what you need. Do not be ashamed to ask for win-win relationships with the people that come to you.

## Times Are about as Good as You Allow Them to Become

In conclusion, times are only as good as your mind perceives them. Just when you think you are failing is the exact moment to continue your gratitude, meditating on your goals and action! That moment of doubt is when the highest good for you is ready to unfold; sometimes people call this grace. Even if the result is not exactly as you want, something better is coming to you at the right time and place. Therefore, you are many times protected from a bad outcome or relationship by waiting a little longer and preparing yourself for a better situation.

# *Thoughts Are Energy and Substance*

## Our Thoughts, Actions, Inactions, and Omissions Create Our Character

Overall, repeated thoughts become tendencies or habits, willingness and willpower can initiate action, and repeated experiences lead to wisdom. Our combined thoughts, actions, inactions, and omissions are what create the totality of our character.

If we desire prosperous and peaceful energy, we must be willing to put out good thoughts, praise others, become thankful, see things in an opportunistic light, and have faith in the regeneration of mind and body. Our every action and thought of goodness is very powerful. Acts of kindness, service to others, and self-development are all extremely powerful energies. Negative feelings are feeble thoughts that are a hundred times less powerful than acts of creation and constructiveness. If we maintain a harmonious relationship with others while keeping a peaceful relationship with ourselves, then life can be much easier. Further, when we are avoiding wasteful thinking and actions, our spiritual energies may maintain their laser focus and power. As with physics, it is possible to neutralize a sound wave by setting up another sound wave of the same pattern that comes from the opposite pole. Therefore it is possible to conjure and visualize ideas, thoughts, and images that can completely neutralize old attitudes. By changing your outlook, you can change your future. Every cause has its effect, and every action has its results, but it is desire that is the link that connects the two. Thinking on a higher level requires a mind that is free, lean, efficient, harmonious, and clear. Gratitude and attunement will afford us the clarity to absorb prosperity and build anew.

## *Get Clarity and Peace*

**Steps of Attunement.** The clearing away of mental debris through a process of self-analysis and attunement will allow us to obtain greater peace of mind and mental effectiveness toward abundance.

1. **Remain Teachable:** Keep right-sized with regard to our ego.
2. **Developing Character:** Seek change and be open to growth. Eliminate what is not useful and adapt for new abilities
3. **Honesty and Integrity:** Do what you say and be honest with yourself.
4. **Purity of Thought:** Keep your thinking clear, act in the now, and enjoy each moment.
5. **Be Selfless:** Give without expectation of return through service and non-hoarding of things and yourself. Circulate your goodness and radiate your excellence.
6. **Develop Higher Purpose:** Making healthy decisions to have a definite purpose toward your objectives or advancement for all.

7. **Appreciation:** Be thankful for the gifts you have received, praising others and blessing your home, family, and world.

8. **Reflection:** Maintain a willingness to engage self-analysis and evaluation for the purposes of growth.

9. **Attunement:** Seek harmony to heal disputes with others through amends, restitution, mental catharsis, character development, and right action.

10. **Visualization:** Use contemplation, prayer, or meditation to enable a mental vision of a fuller life and connection to the universe. Apply constructive meaning to past events.

11. **Open Mind:** Keep the motivation to be open-minded about accepting a state of well-being and peace of mind.

12. **Love and Harmony:** Allow peace and tranquility in your life, and embrace a sincere belief that life is abundant and that love and harmony can be allowed in your life permanently.

## *Use Gratitude to Create Abundance*

Through the development of a mindset of gratitude, we pave the way for a consciousness of expectation of the best. To begin, we comprehend that there is a source of creation from which all things proceed. Second, we believe that cooperating with the universe or the source gives us everything you desire. Third, we relate ourselves to the world with a feeling of deep and profound gratitude. Further, the universe is overflowing with good things, and there is so much of everything that the earnest hunger of every heart can be gratified.

We do not have to take anything from anyone to have true abundance, because there is more than enough for everyone. The fact that someone has abundance does not prove that he has taken some or all of his wealth from others, although this is what a great many believe due to the lack of understanding of the law. The universe is overflowing with abundance; if we do not have everything that we want, there is a reason; there may be some definite cause somewhere, either in ourselves or in our relations to the world. When this cause can be found and corrected, then we may proceed to take possession of advancement.

## Gratitude Brings Your Whole Being into Greater Harmony

Multitudes continue in poverty from no other cause than a lack of gratitude. If it is a new thought that gratitude brings your whole being into closer harmony with the creative energies of the universe, then consider it well and be open to this new and powerful truth. In the past, we may have not stayed in tune with abundance, but we have learned through evidence that connection is the key. Sometimes people make the mistake of cutting the wires that connect them to prosperity by failing to maintain a grateful consciousness. This deficiency can be corrected and cured if you take advantage of this system.

To begin with, the grateful outreaching of your mind in thankful praise to the supreme intelligence is a liberation or expenditure of force; it cannot fail to reach that which it addresses, and the reaction is an instantaneous movement toward you. We are now beginning to realize that the greatest thing in the world is to live closely in tune with the infinite that we constantly feel the power and the peace of the presence. But the value of gratitude does not consist solely in getting us more blessings in the future. Without gratitude, we cannot long keep from harboring dissatisfied thoughts regarding things as they are. We also realize that the more closely we live to the infinite, the more we shall receive of all good things, because all good things have their source in the Supreme—but how to enter into this life of supreme oneness with the Most High is the quest of many seekers. The soul that is always grateful lives nearer the true, the good, the beautiful, and the perfect. The more closely we live to the good and the beautiful, the more we shall receive of all those things.

The grateful mind is constantly fixed upon the best, and therefore it tends to become the best. It takes the form or character of the best and will receive the best. Also, faith is born of gratitude. The grateful mind continually expects good things, and expectation becomes faith. The reaction of gratitude upon one's own mind produces faith, and every outgoing wave of grateful thanksgiving increases faith.

Notice the grateful attitude that Jesus took, and how he always seems to be saying, "I thank thee, Father, that thou hearest me." You cannot exercise much power without gratitude, for it is gratitude that keeps you connected with power. The more grateful we are for the good things that come to us now, the more good things we shall receive in the future. This is a great metaphysical law, and we shall find it most profitable to comply exactly with this law, no matter what the circumstances may be. Be grateful for all gifts, and you will constantly receive more of everything. Thus the simple act of being grateful becomes a path to perpetual increase. The reason for this is that the mental outlook of authentic gratitude will draw you into much closer contact with the power that produces all excellent and good things.

In other words, to be grateful for what we have received is to draw more closely to the source of that which we receive. The good things that come to us arrive because we have properly employed certain laws, and when we are appreciative for the results gained, we enter into more perfect harmony with those laws and thus become able to employ these laws to still greater advantage. Anyone can understand this idea, and those who do not know that gratitude produces this effect should try it and watch the results.

The attitude of gratitude brings the whole mind into more perfect and more harmonious relations with all the laws and powers of life. The grateful mind gains a firmer hold, so to speak, upon those things in life that can produce increase. This concept is simply illustrated in personal experience, where we find that we always feel nearer to that person to whom we express real gratitude. When we thank a person and truly mean it with heart and soul, we feel nearer to that person than we ever did before. Likewise, when we express our earnest thanksgiving to everything and everybody that comes into our lives, we draw closer and closer to all the creative powers of life.

The moment you permit your mind to dwell with dissatisfaction upon things as they are, you begin to lose ground. If you fix attention upon the common, the ordinary, and the poor, then your mind may weaken or be distracted. Therefore the person who has no feeling of gratitude cannot long retain a living faith. In other words, to maintain power we must tap into the real source from which all good things in life proceed.

When we consider this principle from another point of view, we find the act of being grateful is an absolute necessity, if we wish to accomplish as much as we have the power to accomplish. To be grateful in this large, universal sense is to enter into harmony with the highest and the best in life. We thus gain possession of the superior elements of mind and soul. Consequently, we gain the power to become more and achieve more, no matter what our object or work may be. All of this will place us in a more perfect relation with life, enabling us to appropriate the greater richness of life.

## The Grateful Mind Expects Good Things and Will Always Secure Good Things out of Everything

What is gratitude? To be grateful is to think of the best, and therefore the grateful mind keeps the eye constantly upon the best. According to the law of attraction, we grow into the likeness of that which we think of the most. The grateful mind is constantly looking for the best and thus holding attention upon the best and growing daily into the likeness of the best.

The grateful mind expects only good things and will always secure good things out of everything. We can be more easily open to receive the things that we can earnestly anticipate. When we constantly expect to acquire good out of everything, then we cause everything to manifest good toward us. Therefore to the grateful mind, all things will at all times work together for good, and this means perpetual increase in everything that can add to the happiness and the welfare of man. Anyone can prove this idea to be true, and the proper course to pursue is to cultivate the habit of being grateful for every good thing. Give thanks readily to the abundant force for everything, and feel deeply grateful every moment to every living creature.

All things are situated so that they can be of some service to us, and all things at some point have been instrumental in adding to our welfare. Therefore to be just and true, we must express continuous gratitude to everything that has existence. Be thankful to yourself and to every soul in the world, and most important, be thankful to the creative source of all that is. Live in perpetual thanksgiving to the entire world and express the deepest, sincerest, soul-felt gratitude you can feel within whenever something of value comes into your life.

## *Abundance Every Day: ReInventing*

Let us imagine each day is a new birth and a new opportunity to live again and do the right thing. Each night, our past self can be allowed to die out and reincarnate upon the following morning, and we can be born anew. All men and women have the opportunity to change, atone, grow, regenerate, and be reawakened. Reincarnation is the great opportunity of man to start to build where construction has ceased. After a death of the ego-self, which can happen at any moment, the soul can be malleable and in flux; some call it openness or a "moment of clarity." At these times, we may be in this rebirthing and transformational stage much as the caterpillar in the cocoon. Dynamic changes and growth can occur rapidly from this state. Thus our character and spirit can again act rapidly through the laws of desire, purpose, vibration, and attraction.

Then what is the true lesson of reinventing our life? Is it necessary for us to surrender our ego and cooperate with our spiritual side in order to be given another opportunity to build the life that is our higher purpose? If so, how do we accomplish this? This awakening can occur by virtue of a shift of consciousness, a sacramental initiation, a molecular regeneration, a release of negative thinking by private confession, a confirmation of your path, or a rebirth of the spirit.

Reincarnation for the student of the soul is the transmuting of the baser desires and ideals into that fine and pure ideal, and toward a conscious, loving, and peaceful existence. In summary, each day is a new birth and a new opportunity to live again.

## *Process to Create New Opportunity*

» Relax and cultivate oneness with the universal mind or source of all. Recognize that you are part of all and in communion with all.

» Specify exactly what conditions you desire to produce.

» Specify in your mind what you will do with the results of the desire.

» Concentrate thoughts on the desired mental picture.

» Imagine the possibilities with confident expectation.

» There is no need to strain; peacefully allow your thoughts to visualize the highest outcome.

» Do your visualizations with a grateful frame of mind.

» Your mental images are specific, but you should be open to results that are even better than you have specified.

» Mentally remain open to receive and to actually possess the desired condition or result.

» Accept that the condition can be yours and believe that you *have it*.

» After your visualization exercises, go out into the world with your intuition and plans. *Take action*, leaving no stone unturned.

» Simple affirmations can influence your belief. An example is the following: Repeating the word "love," "health," or "wealth" with emotion and with persistence can allow you to live and feel joy.

» Approaching your goals, actions, and mental exercises with enthusiasm and a thankful heart can be a catalyst to your desires.

# *Thoughts on Manifesting Your Desires*

Manifestation is the work of the creative power itself. Gratitude and thankfulness lead to greater constructive expectation in our daily living. Positive expectation and confident expectation is faith. If you repudiate the potential of miracles, they will not materialize in your field of consciousness. Recognize the possibility, and it will appear. Praise others, bless others, and bless and praise yourself and the miracle of your creation. When blended with humility, your connection to source will open a pipeline of grace and supply into your life. A thankful heart is highly conducive to faith, confident expectation, and living with joy. Know forgiveness in your heart; feel that the supreme forgives you. Realize that you are forgiven all transgressions once and for all. With your self-forgiveness, you free your mind's mental and spiritual power. What you think clearly about becomes expansive in your life. Your focus on the good and the great will bring the good and the great into your world.

NOTES

✓ _____

✓ _____

✓ _____

✓ _____

✓ _____

✓ _____

✓ _____

✓ _____

# PART II:

# SECRETS OF SUCCESS TO REFLECT UPON

## *Affirmations to Abundant Success*

1. **We are all connected to the source of creation—** The life force, and nature itself. We are all created of source, but because of our individual consciousness, we each have our own unique spirit or being-ness in concert with the universe.

2. **Our thinking and the focused power of our thoughts can** accelerate or change the direction of the universal forces that apply to us; we are divinely inspired with creative feelings. However, the focus of our habitual thinking draws energy and manifestations from the universe.

3. **Our views and thinking are always present.** Learning how to constructively use our consciousness is the key. Control, discipline, concentration, and focus are skills of mastery that can vastly augment our abilities to be creators. We do have the ability to control our thoughts. Most of us have never tried controlled thinking or directed thought.

4. **If we are determined to become "self-reliant,"** the universe will recognize this decision of response-ability, and it will begin to cooperate with and help us.

5. **We must also befriend the world and embrace it**. When we begin to cooperate with supreme intelligence, we begin to flow with the currents of the world where harmonious results begin to occur almost like magic. . This mental action toward a thankful, loving, and peaceful relationship with the source will allow us to: request, ask, receive, and manifest prosperity much more easily.

6. **Abundance comes in many forms,** such as health, ideas, creativity, right work, love, relationships, natural expression of our talents, and even economic success.

7. **Developing a consciousness of being worthy of prosperity** is critically important. We must know that the world wants to lavish us with creativity, happiness, and health. We must that we are blessed with the strength and knowledge that will help us grow and reap abundance.

8. **We can practice giving sincere thanks** for our gifts and feel abundance for any prosperity that we have ever received. Our outpouring of thanks and gratitude can open the portals of the universe to shower us with health, love, peace, and wealth.

9. **Affirming our good and our harmonious connection to the world** can also create worthiness and a thankful heart. Tune in with the life force and use the spoken word to affirm what you want from the spirit.

10. **Spirit is love, peace, and harmony**. When you think from a perspective of love, peace, and harmony while making requests to the supreme, your requests will be tens of times more powerful than any other base thought of negative tendency. Concentrate upon your mental requests for abundance with thanksgiving. Bless and praise your

body, your health, your world, your successes, and your gifts, and the world will begin to bless and praise you in return.

11. **We must learn to graduate from hope to belief**. Move from wishing to the certainty of faith and transform your mindset toward a state of confident knowing.

12. **We must obtain the habit of** realization **of the divine presence**. This unity is many times more powerful that any sense of separateness.

13. **Our clarity and awareness become greater with unity** toward the supreme. Our alertness and curiosity grows more profound with gratitude and harmony. We are more inundated with ideas, creative thoughts, and greater dreams of growth with awareness and inquisitiveness.

14. **The powers of attraction have several vital points**. Reinventing yourself and your personal attributes is different from the concept of wanting a tangible thing. Regarding attracting and changing our character, we can expand our outlook each day toward an ideal or objective. As an example, if we want to become an expert in a specific field such as sports or teaching, we think of these things, feed ourselves with the ideas related to these fields, act the part, learn the part, and be the part. We act as if we are what we desire. In order to become, we must internalize in mind and heart that which we seek, as well as mastering the external knowledge, experiences, and facets of the art.

15. **We should also learn to use the law of attraction with the manifestation of objects**. With things or forms, you must also see yourself as being the person who would have the thing that you desire. Thus, you are seeing yourself in possession of

and utilizing something that you have declared, specified, mentally pictured, and visualized. It will be vitally important to emotionalize the mental pictures with an earnest and sincere belief of the possession of it. The desire is energized by having commingled the mental images of having the desired outcome together with the emotions of joy, appreciation, and thanks.

16. **We can pre-dream with sincerity and positive emotion**. We can allow our ideas of the future to be pushed into the universal field of the formless and to begin to coalesce forward to formation. This experience is similar to remembering a past event: the past happened, but it can seem like a dream. We can imagine our plans into manifestation day by day. This is potentiality in action.

17. **We are all in thought:** what we think earnestly into "in our mind" is taken up and done unto us. This means that as we think with heartfelt, constructive faith, it will be done. We cannot think one way one day and change our thought the next, and hope to get the desired results. We must be very clear in our ideas, sending out such continuous thoughts as we wish to see manifested in our condition.

18. **We are conceiving sensory impressions all day, every day**. Sometimes our constructive daydreaming is great and wonderful, and when a new idea becomes thought consuming, we can take a sincere look at our inspiration and determine if this idea requires our boldness, analysis, and action. If it does, we can begin to think into it—we can conceive it, better comprehend it, affirm it, and begin to know it mentally.

19. **Either the truth of an idea will begin to appear quickly,** or we can let it go. If it becomes a burning

SPIRITUAL WEALTH MANAGEMENT

desire, we will begin to earnestly feel the possibility of the new: idea, health, abundance, or prosperity with certainty.

20. **Remember to embody and feel consciously what you want and desire**. Become it and be it. Enjoy the thoughts and expectations of creation and transformation.

21. **Avoid toxic energy**, and avoid people who are blaming or always negative. You would not expose yourself to a deadly toxin or germ if you could avoid it. Thus you must be a prudent steward of your mind, spirit, and body.

22. **Focus your mind on becoming your best** and moving toward your highest expression of life. Learn to be your best!

23. **Find someone of excellence you want to model yourself after.** If you have trouble imagining the best and begin to copy the character, path, education, habits, and success of a person who represents the best. Then, continue to surround yourself with those who are enthusiastic about life and learn to believe in the inherent goodness of the world.

24. **Encircle yourself with those who are already rich in life**, full of spirit, and eager for knowledge.

25. **Associate with those who are pulling for you**, are supportive of your dreams, and believe in your potential. Bless and support their dreams in return.

26. **Don't say things that decry the good will** of the universe

27. **Learn to refute: hate, anger, poverty, and other ills**—they are none of your concern. Become all you can and work to improve your health, mind, and

prosperity. Then, your new power can help all those you choose with your secrets and success.

28. **All is right with your world** because you are centered in gratitude, harmony, action, and good will. Because you are strong and working to maintain your balance, you are constantly increasing and growing in prosperity.

29. **We cannot afford to find fault or to focus on the wrongs of the world**. The God of Love cannot hear the prayer of the man who is not representative of love who does not speak the language with love. Love and cooperation will be found to be the greatest business principle on earth: God is love.

30. **Find what is right with the world**, and focus on what is good. Your confidence and strength can be built much more easily with this newfound focus and concentration, and your attention and focus will be more laser-focused if you seek to find what is right with the world.

31. **If you look for what is right with the world,** you will continue to find it with ease. Finding things to be grateful for will allow you to develop a thankful heart. Faith and knowingness become relatively easy with the cultivated ability for heartfelt appreciation and praise.

# PART III:

# EXERCISES

Each of these mental exercises are designed to help you with your powers of abundance. These short examples will expand your senses, your perception, your awareness, and your abilities to concentrate.

## *Perception and Awareness Exercise*

1. Sit in a relaxed position.
2. Relax each section of the body and take a few deep breaths.
3. Imagine a warm, creative energy radiating through your body.
4. Enter what we call the alpha state, which is relaxed daydreaming of the right brain.
5. Begin to feel or sense each part of the body.
6. Direct your attention to your toes or hands or ears. Notice how each part of the body feels.
7. Now close your eyes and notice any sounds either of your body or around you.
8. See if you can hear something far away.
9. Now, refocus and imagine just one sound or image.
10. Focus all of your thought on seeing, hearing, feeling, tasting, or smelling what you have imagined.
11. Imagine a part of the scene or object the exclusion of everything else. As an example, try to imagine

just the sound of a soft trumpet or French horn playing a song.

12. After a few minutes, relax again and come back to your beta state of mind and consciousness, the left brain.

## *An Exercise for Intuition and Guidance*

1. Engage in the following steps:
   » Sit in a relaxed position.
   » Relax each part of the body from top to bottom and take a few deep breaths.
   » Imagine a warm energy radiating through your body.
2. With eyes closed, see yourself going into a sacred castle.
3. As you enter the main chamber of the castle, you see the helpful person of your choice. This imaginary guide or person could be alive, from the past, or your spiritual self.
4. You then talk with her or him in your mind's eye. [Imagination.] and feel free to ask questions directly to your chosen guide, and you then allow your spiritual guide to answers these questions.
5. Listen deeply to your heart and intuition. Try and sense the answers from your core. [heart and stomach.]
6. When you are finished, thank your guide for the help and direction.
7. You may have an overwhelming sense that the voice or messages of the guide come from a higher viewpoint than your own. If so, consider it well and be mindful of your intuition.

# *An Exercise for Energy and Healing*

1. Sit in a relaxed position. Relax each section of the body and take a few deep breaths. Imagine a warm, creative energy radiating through your body. Enter what we call the alpha state, which is relaxed daydreaming of the right brain. While relaxing in a chair with spine straight, rest your hands on your lap.
2. Close your eyes and visualize a peaceful lake that has no ripples. Then see yourself surrounded by bright white particles of energy that permeate your body.
3. In your mind, see the healing, bright light move toward any area of bodily discomfort. Allow this white light to fill any affected area and flow thought your body. Know that the white light brings all of your body's healing power to work most effectively for you.
4. Take a few deep breaths.
5. Allow this bright light to act like flowing water, purifying and washing your entire body.
6. Feel and see in your mind's eye that the washing waves of white light are pure love which immunizes you to any and all fear, resentment, hurt, and disease.
7. Say to yourself, "I forgive myself and everyone for the past."
8. Thank the light of the universe for removing any impurities from your body.

9. Claim mental freedom from all problems in your mind and spirit. Thank the universe for your expanding health and peace.
10. See others in your mind's eye walking up to you and congratulating you on your healing and success.
11. That's it … so open your eyes.
12. You can also send this light to another who needs healing.

## 3 Exercises for Gratitude

» Get in a quiet place where there are no distractions and think of the alphabet. Think of a letter—select the letter "J," for instance. Think of a person in your family or in your childhood with a "J" in his or her name whom you were very fond of or even loved. Ponder that loving emotion; think of the happy times you had with this person. Bless that person in your mind. Consider the ability to transfer this feeling to another person whom you want to bless today.

» Think of a color—for example, blue. Think of something blue that you owned that gave you happiness in the past. Harvest that emotion and feel it. Try to mentally recapture the joy of having the experience.

» Consider one of the five senses (taste, touch, smell, hearing, seeing). Select one, such as smell. Remember your favorite aroma, and think back about the flavor or pleasant smell. Ponder the joys of enjoying that aroma again—for example, a great cup of espresso in Venice, Italy. Experience the moments in the past that you enjoyed in conjunction with the feeling and senses. Allow gratitude to fill the mind, spirit, and body.

# *Exercise for Harmony*

Consider the following several methods to achieve inner harmony and to be in tune with spiritual abundance.

» Start blessing and praising what is yours.

» Harvest a thankful heart and mind for all of your good fortune, such as the ability to do simple things like thinking, tasting, smelling, hearing, seeing, and more.

» Get into nature or a quiet place to be still. Allow your mind and heart to be open. Visualize an open space or a wide but empty green meadow.

» Take a moment to sit or kneel and make a prayer of thanksgiving.

» Write out a list of things for which you are thankful, and keep them in your wallet to read whenever you need to refocus on how you are truly blessed and protected by the universe.

» Limit complaining and begin praising or complimenting others. *Start at home.*

» Think of a person who has been truly kind to you.

» Try to remember a person who you think really loves you.

» Think of all those who love or care for you now.

» Do something for another person to help him or her, or simply write the person a letter, or give him or her a flower.

» Spend time with a spouse, loved one, or child, and focus only on wonderful, beautiful, encouraging thoughts about this person.

## *See Yourself in Your Mind's Eye*

» See yourself doing what you want to do. Imagine a labor of love.

» See yourself living where you want to live.

» See yourself fulfilled in your relationships.

» Act, feel, and think as if you are who you want to be. This will assist in the growth and enhancement of your total character in reaching spiritual abundance.

» Envision yourself in the occupation of your dreams. What would it be like? How would you feel?

» Harvest the emotion of having all you desire. The mind's eye is the picture screen of creation: the more clearly and powerfully you project your images in and onto your consciousness and then to your subconscious, the easier it will be for your ideals and goals to manifest.

As a strategy, imagine exactly what you want with specificity. Imagine successfully earning the best outcome. Then project that image and feeling into the world, like sending out a letter. Imagine the exact, completed, successful outcome. You can do this exercise anytime and each day until you have achieved your desired consciousness of success and prosperity.

# PART IV:

# CHANGING, KNOWING, AND BECOMING

## What Every Spiritual Seeker Should Know

Regardless of your culture and traditions, personal character growth and seeking a higher purpose are goals toward which we should aspire. When we analyze and become a student of history, we can see leaders who have utilized the proven keys to peace and prosperity. These strategies are rooted in nearly all the schools of ancient mystery teachings of this world. In the prophetic quest of a higher order, it becomes evident that these success strategies are tethered to many common denominators. From the first cuneiform texts of Sumer and Babylon to the teachings of oriental or American shamans, these wisdom manuscripts enlighten the seeker with shared key instructions in spirituality and metaphysics.

Like our ancient forefathers, people today still look to invoke the power of the universe and seek to communicate or harmonize with the Supreme. We need only to look toward the stars and the heavens to imagine the possibility of boundless universal forces of the cosmos. The greatest human minds have speculated upon the divine forces and our spiritual potential from the times of Pythagoras and Socrates to the present day. Spiritual masters, world leaders, religious gurus, and even today's CEOs have learned to incorporate contemplation and metaphysical exercises in their daily routine; in doing so, they optimize their inner peace and outer success. These enlightened souls are successful individuals with an unspoken vow to expand their spiritual mindset and achieve maximum performance and tranquility.

## Engaging Metaphysics

Understanding the fundamentals of metaphysics can be the key to great success. Metaphysics is a branch of philosophy concerned with explaining the fundamental nature of being. Philosophers from Socrates to Kant and to Benjamin Franklin have all offered teachings and best practices to expand potentiality. We have have all had periods of mind and body evolution; sometimes we grow swiftly, and other times we incrementally grow. As young adults the focus is on practical learning and bodily growth. Then there is the pure enjoyment of reaching adulthood and learning about life, which can be a fearless initiation rite. Shortly after our college age years, we begin to see the sheer importance of balance. Then we learn that we must define our direction and goals and make real commitments; otherwise we may feel that we will fall behind. We ask ourselves, What do we want most? Is it possible to have it all? Can we enjoy long-lasting health, peace, wealth, freedom, and independence? Can we develop the ability to adapt effectively to life's ups and downs? For anybody to achieve wholeness and peace of mind, the individual must seek to be balanced on spiritual, mental, and physical levels.

One thing is for certain: our thought generally precedes all of our actions and growth. More importantly, we can creatively direct our intentions. Here are some questions to contemplate.

» *Do you have great ideas?*
» *Do you follow your dreams?*
» *Do you finish things?*
» *When do creative ideas come to you?*
» *Do you write down your thoughts?*

## Reinvention and Renewal of Character

While growing up, many of us are paralyzed by fears of failure. How do we get past this? For many, getting past the possibility of failure can be overcome by considering the worst that could happen while imagining the best results, too. This is where thinking about the best results and outcomes is important. We must develop an attitude of expecting the best. When we expect the best, we grow in that character and direction. Let's face it—the cosmic cards of joy, excellence, and achievement are stacked in our favor when we are living and thinking in constructive ways. The question becomes, what would we do if we could not fail?

Some folks are challenged by worthiness issues, too. Many of us have not developed that inner character of confidence and poise. How do we grow a healthy self-regard? What strategies will facilitate a positive change in our beliefs about ourselves? For many, getting to the point where we believe in ourselves and abilities is a huge transformation. We all have the potential for great things; we should be able to become what we want. As unique individuals we are all important, and so are our creations, services, products, ideas, work, and efforts. We must make sure that we hold out ourselves and our services as valuable to all involved. Learn to articulate what you do with a sense of purpose and enthusiasm.

Giving praise is sometimes overlooked, yet outward blessings always seem to be returned to us in abundance. Are you open to receiving and giving gifts, praise, and compliments? Your openness to receive the gifts of life is also critical, and you should allow your mind to be ready to receive prosperity, quality relationships, health, and accomplishments.

While you think of your goals and objectives, decide how you will receive them and utilize the blessings that come to you. Make sure you have a method and plan to use and capture the prosperity that will be sent to you by others and the generous universe in which we live.

## Adapting and Change

Change is sometimes very difficult, but we can also realize the fruits of personal growth through a process of adaptation. We each already have some unique talents, and genius comes in a multitude of forms. For efficiency, it is sometimes best to focus our goals where we can use some of our preexisting talents. A goal that already has our interest and enthusiasm will be much more achievable. To naturally express our talents is where we perform on a level of comfort, passion, and excellence. Inevitably there comes a time where we must surrender to the possibility of change and innovation and move toward our true place or destiny.

It is said that necessity is the mother of invention. While getting out of our comfort zone is difficult, we are compelled to seek new choices and renewed action. It is in our nature to seek to grow toward abundance.

On a deeper level, do you feel there is something better? Are you willing to take action? Are you taking responsibility for your life today and planning for the future. Is your purpose calling to you to make advancement toward your joyous intentions? A key figure of German literature, von Goethe inferred that boldness is sometimes required, and it can be the nucleus of a new beginning and genius.

Before taking action, you may require proper articulation and clear planning. Writing may be the key to expanding your consciousness and purpose. Do you write out what you want? Do you take time out each week or month to quietly plan or meditate over your ideals, goals, purpose, objectives, or happiness? Writing can be intricate, but remember that when we write, this exercise can energize untapped forces that work to help us expand our vision.

Getting into the flow can also create efficiencies and dramatic growth and peace. Many of us have experienced a situation in which we resist a decision or process. Sometimes we can alter our mental state and become more in tune with flow. Using the timeless allegory, floating down a river can be very easy as compared to swimming upstream. Similar to the theory of detaching, we must also allow the world to co-create with us, and we need to accept the best outcomes. Remember, there are times to review facts, analyze a situation, seek insight, take corrective action, and to allow your good to unfold.

## Get the Blueprint: Metaphysics and Planning

To advance toward your purpose may require ongoing and updated specificity. Each of us needs to clarify our desires, ideals, and thoughts. When was the last time you were really specific and itemized the tasks necessary to achieve your objectives? If there is someone with the power to help you, were you able to ask another person for help or for what you wanted? Were you willing to earn it? When was the last time that you expressed yourself to others in such a way that your passion and heart was in back of your clear and unequivocal desires?

Can you make a choice and move forward? Can you move ahead and not look back? After you make a commitment, can you utilize emotions as a vital force in energizing your goals? Similarly, can you clarify the essence in back of your choice? The essence is the rationale behind your objective and desires—that is, to serve humanity or solve a problem. An amazing combination of force comes into being when our choices are backed with essence, purpose, and enthusiasm.

» What is the reason in back of your desire?
» How will it serve humanity?
» How will you use the result?
» Are your commitments energized?
» What would be your ideal life?
» What makes you feel alive, what gives you joy?
» Can you associate your aliveness and joy toward your true purpose or career in life?

GEORGE S MENTZ JD MBA CWM

There are a multitude of occupations that involve the creation of products and services that improve the lives of others. Most people never sit down with themselves, those they trust, or their family to discuss exactly what they would like to do. Each person's goals or personal "peace of mind" may be different and subjective. If we can spend some time to write out things that interest us, it always helps clear a path for greater ideas, focus, and direction.

While you develop your mission and purpose, you may want to evaluate your psychological efficiency level and determine whether you have mental blocks or fears of success, happiness, and peace.

>> *What may be blocking you?*
>> *Have you taken responsibility for your life and choices?*
>> *Is there something that you need to let go of?*
>> *Can you transcend blame and excuses?*
>> *Do you believe that great opportunity is possible?*

## Practicing Excellence: Growing Character

If you have bad habits that are holding you back, you may already know what they are. Just thinking about the possibility of constructive change is an improvement. Thinking about what it would be like without the negative impact of a nonproductive habit is a powerful exercise. Envisioning the benefits of being free of the negative practice is invigorating.

## The Mental Architecture

Contemplation and meditation may be the key to focusing your attention upon the most constructive ideas Here are some questions to consider..

>> *Can you practice using your mind's eye?*
>> *Can you see or visualize improvement, adaptation, and the manifestation of your goals?*

» *Can you project upon your own mental picture screen the things you want in life in detail.*
» *Can you project what you want in color, with sound and with detail, while feeling the emotions of success?*
» *Do you believe in your ideas with faith and knowingness?*
» *Do you protect your ideas from ignorance?*
» *Can you keep your rapid spiritual growth confidential while working toward personal improvement and success?*
» Can you make affirmations, prayers or petitions?
» Are you willing to think or speak to your subconscious about what you want from life?

You exist, and therefore you have the ability to think. Your spirit is your essence. When you say, "I am healthy, whole, complete, and perfect," this means that the God in you is also perfect. The knowingness of this proclamation is very liberating.

During our journey in life, people are always sent to help us. When we are in tune with a higher purpose while maintaining inner peace, our worldview and energy will attract the right people from around the world to help us. It is our duty to decide whether to engage them or meet them half way.

Our mind is an amazing processor—a register of facts, senses, pictures, and plans. The mind works on the ideas and images that it receives. When you want something to be brought into your world, you can mentally visualize a successful result.

Every major success is preceded by an imagined blueprint, practice, or plan. The pattern of what we feed our consciousness develops the character of our thinking and action. What we continually feed our conscious can influence our deeper ideas and beliefs.

## Awareness

Each of us needs to keep our perception open to creation. Our opportunities and ideas will come to us each day : people may bring up fresh insights, or some new event or statement may jolt your consciousness to take new action. We need to be mindful of our environment and keep our focus while maintaining awareness to our surroundings. Being contemplative while in action is the key. Being consciously aware allows us to see, learn, grow, and experience the moment.

## Using Gratitude and Enthusiasm to Energize Life

**Thanksgiving.** Whatever we bless, we expand in our life. Whatever we are thankful for will also manifest more freely into our world. A thankful heart and mind can augment our perception from limited possibilities into a faith with unlimited opportunity. We need to remain open to new ideas, living life fully, and keeping a healthy detachment from the fast-moving insanity of our high-tech world.

**Reaping.** The law of sowing and reaping is a simple method of growing abundance in our personal life. It can be said that giving, tithing, and circulation are the opposite of hoarding. When we circulate energy or money, the floodgates of opportunity can be opened for us.

Although all of us become comfortable with our routines, we need to continue to grow. As Socrates implied, personal analysis is the key to knowing oneself. This applies to the individual and to the organization as we need to learn from our successes and failures. As an example, Benjamin Franklin would work toward continuous improvement of his character in his daily inventory, prayers, and meditations. As with any business inventory, there comes a time where we must discard the old and make room for the new; we must prune the tree at times to afford even greater expansion.

Remember that love and praise are the fuel that makes our world come alive. People will do just about anything for praise and recognition. True leaders and successful people understand that compliments, gratitude, praise, and other acts of recognition of others create loyalty, respect, gratitude, and even loving relationships. Thus there is a time where we all must lay well-earned praise on others, our family, our staffs, and even upon ourselves.

## Chapter Conclusion

On a more practical level, many of the objectives that we will want to achieve will involve a step-by-step approach and fundamental processes. This methodology will usually include an investigation, diagnosis, analysis, benchmarking, modeling, planning, action individual tasks, implementation, monitoring, and continuous improvement. In urgent situations, we will call upon all of what we know to do our best in any emergency, but most of the important issues are long-term ideals where we have time to prepare. Similar to project management or wealth management practices, these steps are general in nature and involve many sub-tasks and sub-activities. These activities may also relate to the tenets of various cultural and historical philosophical terms such as perception, higher potential, efficient action, articulation and communication, understanding and listening, concentration, gratitude, effort, action, contemplation, and focus.

## Ingredients for Results
    » Cultivating ideas and desires
    » Doing your homework
    » Asking for information and help
    » Believing in your possibility
    » Taking action
    » Maintaining enthusiasm and expecting the best

## NOTES

✓ _____
✓ _____
✓ _____
✓ _____
✓ _____
✓ _____
✓ _____
✓ _____

# Why Remain a Student of Prosperity?

» To maintain serenity and a state of well being.
» To unwind and unplug from the world and to refocus on being your best, expressing your best, and reaping the great riches of the world.
» To take time for self-analysis, evaluate our progress, and plan.
» To learn from others about topics of interest on relationships, family, business, or success.
» To be involved in group learning and discussions.
» To interrupt the ego and refocus on what is important.
» To learn how to move toward your purpose or life's goals.
» To challenge ourselves regarding our thinking, actions, or even insanity.

The development of a prosperity consciousness can help people build up a new awareness as to what is important in life. These timeless principles tend to allow earnest seekers to break up preconceptions of scarcity and limitations, to open their minds to wealth and success. If the ideas can create willingness for change, they may interrupt one's old thinking and create a desire for change and growth. This clarity is preferred so that the postulant can muster a change in viewpoint or find a call to action for new enthusiasm in life.

Many of these concepts may help people get an honest look at themselves for the very first time. With diligent self-analysis, students may find exactly what is holding them back without clinging to blame. Others may have other breakthroughs to transcend victimhood and go beyond the desire for sympathy.

The overall goal of these strategies is to promote personal effectiveness and allow people to overcome mental barriers. By breaking through, you become free to live and to take action while developing a new awareness.

Learning how to accept life events, putting the past behind, and getting out of comfort zones are all major themes of these carpe-diem–focused teachings. If people who seek greater opportunity can become open to action and possibilities in the now, they may soon learn to experience a richer and fuller life with authentic experiences.

Are you interpreting your life in constructive ways? Are you a man or woman of your word? Are you the type of person who does what you say you will do? The reality of your integrity score must be seen objectively. We may all benefit from taking a sincere look at our truth and history. The room for improvement in our lives can be great.

An moment of clarity can occur quickly by realizing that self-transformation is an inside job. "Inside job" implies the necessity for change of the individual and not the environment;

the change that is required can be of mental, physical, and spiritual dimension. Over the past years, your track record of your life's experience has probably been the direct result, or the sum total, of your actions, thinking, and omissions. Thus without revised action of mind and body, the record or path cannot change.

Like transcendentalism or ancient Taoism, authenticity is most closely linked to your natural expression.

1. We must take earnest action to become who we are meant to be.
2. We must avoid blame and victimhood, and focus on building up ourselves to rise to greater heights.
3. We must conform to the rules of the game but allow ourselves to remain true to our authentic side. If remaining true to ourselves forces us to move outside of the mainstream, then that may be required.
4. We must get past our ego and remain teachable to acquire growth.
5. We must enjoy the now, take action in the now, but respect the past and plan to be our best in the future.

# PART V:

# DEVELOPING A CONSCIOUSNESS OF SUCCESS AND ABUNDANCE

We earnestly urge upon you to cultivate a spiritual-based consciousness that you may realize the unique, everlasting power within you. The real individual spirit concealed behind the mask of personality is you, the real self, the "I,"– and that part of you that is conscious when you say "I am," which is your assertion of existence and latent power. Remember, the "I" exists independent of the body. Power and life comes from the very center of one's being—the "I am" region of our heart, mind, and consciousness. With a realization of the true self comes a sense of power that will manifest through you and make you strong. The awakening to a realization of the "I" in its clearness and vividness will cause you to feel a sense of being and power that you have never before known, and then there will come naturally to you the correlated consciousness that expresses itself in the statement, "I can and I am willing"—one of the grandest affirmations of power that man can make. This "I can and will" consciousness is that expression of the something within, which you will realize and manifest. I feel that behind all the advice that I can give you, this one thing is the prime factor in the secret of success. You can always get a better running start when you're already in action, which will give you an advantage over the best standing start imaginable. Get into action and motion. I have endeavored to call your attention to something of far greater importance than a mere code of rules and general advice.

I have pointed out to you the glorious fact that within each of you there is a special something within, which when aroused would give you a greatly increased power and capacity. And so I have tried to tell you this story of the something within, from different viewpoints, so that you might catch the idea in several ways. I firmly believe that success depends most materially upon a recognition and manifestation of this something within.

**Please review the following concepts.**
1. The universal force of God wants us to be happy, successful, and healthy, and to have a rich, abundant, and full life.
2. Your subconscious mind has powers that can be influenced by your conscious mind. Consistently making constructive impressions on your subconscious mind will soon change your thinking, your energy, your effectiveness, and your vibration.
3. Rejoice and be exceedingly glad that the universe has blessed you, your family, your ideas, and your actions.
4. Everything that touches your life is an opportunity, if you discover its proper use. Be aware of each circumstance and study them all, for they are your opportunities. Most men fail by hoping for some particular kind of luck, instead of being ready to seize every opportunity.
5. If there is lack in our lives, we need only to think and do something about it to improve our lot in life. Real change of character may be sought out.
6. Money is only a medium of exchange, and currency is only a symbol of prosperity, much like sheep or cattle have been in the past.
7. Believe that money is not the root of all evil, unless you worship money in and of itself, which we all

know is a violation of the laws of abundance. Peace of mind, balance, harmony, right mind, right action, and right livelihood will invariably lead to richness of life, which includes wealth in many forms (e.g., health and happiness).

8.  Success and money should be used to constructively serve your expansion and humanity. Thus the intention and essence of wealth must be known and directed in a manner that is good for all.

9.  Believe that wealth is a state of mind, and that the consciousness of poverty is not useful for anyone. Therefore a change in consciousness to that of wealth and prosperity can indeed open the doors for ideas, opportunity, and blessings from the Universe.

10. We should commune with universal mind and claim mentally and verbally that spirit will bless us into prosperity.

11. Believe that Spiritual Source is the origin of all wealth. Thus if we realize and connect to that source, our life and path will be abundant.

12. Desire is a power-seeking expression. You cannot desire what is not potentially within you, and therefore you can be what you want to be.

13. Desire is the result of feeling, and a feeling results from a burning desire which is a supernatural faculty, seeking and demanding greater expression.

14. Believe that concentrated thought charged with heart-felt emotion or feelings will almost certainly manifest our desires over time.

15. When man operates on a level of thought that is harmonious and constructive, spiritual forces will positively respond to our mind and actions.

16. Whatever the mind dwells upon will expand and multiply in your life. Whatever the mind praises, blesses, and is thankful for will increase in our life.

17. Love is the most powerful feeling or spirit energy. However, positive prayers, praise, thankfulness, gratitude, and peace are also just as powerful when continuously directed toward an objective such as a relationship, job, or goal.

18. Release your petitions to the universe. Think it, feel it, claim it, mentally have it, and mentally project it on your subconscious picture screen—but then *release* it with a sense of detachment, faith, and confidence where you know that the highest good and outcome will unfold.

19. Be a strong advocate of blessing those of whom we would otherwise be jealous. Thus if somebody is doing well or becoming successful, then we should mentally and verbally praise them, whether friend or foe. The crux of this strategy is to think prosperity without offsetting your vibration with lesser thoughts of ego, fear, and envy.

20. A person who has seen, in their imagination, the end result of any goal has effectively willed the means (the seed) to the realization of the end. It is up to us to cultivate the seed from that juncture. See writings of: Judge Thomas Troward

21. Use constructive affirmations and *know* in our heart with emotion that the affirmation is true. We must consciously commune with the spirit of abundance so as to transmute individual character and consciousness for the better.

22. Believe that man's subconscious or inner spirit is the root of self-enhancing power and the vital connection to spiritual abundance. We can be lifted to new heights by certain constructive habits

and dominant thoughts. One should muster the mind energy to will dominant thoughts over self-defeating ones.

23. Affirm what the heart, mind, and subconscious mind is willing to accept, and then grow the essence of acceptance in a manner to prevent contradiction of mind. Thus, use statements that you can accept with minimal doubt, such as, "I am getting better and better," or, "My income or business sales are increasing every day." As time goes on, affirmations can be expanded.

24. Moreover, each day relax the body, mind, and spirit before making petitions to your subconscious. After entering into a relaxed and peaceful state, you should use affirmations and visualizations with specificity, and send them into the world using focused contemplation.

25. Use the teachings of Jesus (or the prime teacher of your faith) to emphasize that we do not need to live in the illusion of lack and poverty. There is plenty for all, and the universe will simply create more for everyone when we are operating from a spiritual angle.

26. Engage the mindset of opulence. Imagine the end result of your short-term or long-term desires. Feel that it is your true reality *right now* and rejoice in it. Claim it as yours in mind.

27. Reject what seems to be based only on apparent reality. Try to see beyond what your mind of lack wants you to see. Try to see the good in all, not just the inconvenience of a present, past, or future event.

28. Your outer world is directly correlated to your inner thinking. Thus we should try to correct any error

thought and improve the quality of our thinking and spirit connection.

29. We should use prayer or quiet reflection to cleanse our mind and spirit of self-defeating thoughts, and we must quit using destructive thoughts or the past as an excuse not to succeed.

30. Steadily hold the picture of all that you want to attain in person, property, and environment; form a clear conception of it. Then, understand that insofar as your desires are not contrary to eternal justice, it is absolutely certain that you can be what you want to be. Dwell upon your goal and ideal until it is clear and definite to you, and hold it until it arouses intense desire.

31. Pray with unfaltering grateful faith to the supreme intelligence that blessings shall come to you, and thank the supreme in every prayer, petition, or affirmation. Express thanksgiving in every meditation from a heart full of gratitude that your desire is coming to you.

32. Think about this picture until you are always conscious of it. Synergize your desire and send it forth to the universe.

33. As for relationships, students should pray for others. We will have great relationships when we are spiritually whole, happy, and at peace. Moreover, we will attract greater relationships of love and trust when we become better persons filled with self-love, confidence, poise, and joy through the spirit of attraction.

34. We should not allow fear, doubt, and commentary from others blemish our new and improved mental outlook.

35. As an exercise, stand in the mirror and affirm health, wealth, peace, and success for amazing

results. Keep doing this and see how your higher consciousness of prosperity increases your vitality and happiness.

36. One of the best exercises is the use of mental allegory. Thus, students can visualize themselves being congratulated for achieving some wonderful result, objective, or dream.

37. Desire for everybody what you desire for yourself, and be sure to take nothing from anybody without giving a full equivalent in life and value; the more you give, the better for you.

38. Move in absolute faith (harmonious expectation) that all you need for the fullest life that you are capable of living will come to you.

39. Remember that living abundantly consists of continuously increasing life; there is no other way to live. Growth, prosperity, and the ability to innovate, create, and adapt is your birthright.

40. Use each day to the fullest and do each act efficiently and effectively. You must put the abundant thought in everything you do and communicate expansion to all with whom you deal. In this way, others believe that their life will expand by cooperating with you.

41. You must do all that is necessary to advance with today's business, and each day we can build upon that work and faith.

42. Know that people from around the world desire to help you. You are to cooperate and should be willing to receive this mutually beneficial exchange and assistance from those who are sent to you.

43. The basic element of success is to hold the thought and the mental attitude of advancement; and to more than fill your present place. Your advancing thought of increase and win-win mind activity radiates to others and to the supreme force.

44. Use your free time to hone your skills, improve your knowledge, and prepare for your dreams and goals. Do not wait for the perfect opportunity to be all that you want to be. Become all that you can today, and when an opportunity to be more is offered to you, be ready to take it.

45. Use your place or present business as the means of growth, and use your present environment as the means of getting into a better one. Your vision of the right business, if held with faith and purpose, will cause the supreme to move the right occupation toward you. Your action, if performed in the certain way, will cause you to move toward the business.

46. Strive to maintain unity and atonement ("At-One-Ment") with the creative source though your mental expressions of gratitude in your daily life.

47. It can be said that a master of success principles has become spiritually awaken from the state of illusions. When effectively working the steps herein, the practitioner's awareness can be opened where they are in tune with the infinite. When a person opens his eyes, mind, senses, and heart to opportunity, life, bliss, creation and love, the world can blossom before his eyes each waking day. Instead of waking up believing in doom and gloom, the practitioner is waking up expecting the cooperation of the world, universe, and spirit. While recognizing the source of the power, the master also manages his thoughts and mental vibration so as to radiate only the best energy.

48. Remember, your force and energy are yours to protect and strengthen. Don't let others tap into it and try and drain you. Through these principles, you see that your energy can be augmented.. Other people, who do not understand your force,

may carry negative energy or particles that can enter your wave or field. You understand that your mental and spiritual focus on strength, happiness, success, prosperity, health, faith, and confidence will keep your field strong. However, some people may carry particles that are somewhat negative; some examples are complainers, fear mongers, and pessimists. The only way for you to deal with these people is to convey your optimism, avoid them, or neutralize them with thoughts and feelings of love, compassion, and peace. Never bother fighting them—simply allow them to be. All is right with your world, and you need not try to change them in any drastic manner. Your action, faith, character, and prosperity will eventually gain their attention and respect.

49. As with probabilities, each person may have many destinations but engage only one plane of the journey at a time. Thus, actions can put you on a new road of possibilities in the chain of causation. Knowing how to maneuver the energies and opportunities in the external world will allow you to make positive and constructive choices on your path.

50. As it is said, faith is an expectation of something better on a daily basis. Faith involves confidence and resolve over your constructive beliefs. As an example, scientists say that the earth has magma at its core, but nobody has ever been to earth's center; we just take it as fact.

51. The spiritual master knows that pure spirit is at the core of the source of all there is, based on their experience and working with the art of cooperating with the source of all. In the same way, every person of intellect knows that bad germs and parasites

can destroy an unhealthy host. Scientists also know that there are healthy forms of inner agents such as white blood cells or other natural immunities. Therefore the master understands how to attract healthy agents, and also how to become immune to unhealthy forces by neutralizing them by entering the fourth dimension of peace, love, confidence, and prosperity.

52. Understanding the energy of other beings or forces allows the spiritual master to interrelate on this earthly plane in the most effective manner, without harm. The person who best employs these secrets will reach heightened awareness and keep a calm focus on their purpose, using their powers effectively each day. The end result is prosperity, health, harmony, growth, and peace.

53. Gratitude and thankfulness lead to greater constructive expectation in our daily living. Positive and confident expectations are faith. Repudiate miracles and you will receive none. Recognize possibility and it will appear. Praise others, bless others, and bless and praise yourself and the miracle of your creation.

54. Blended with humility, your harmonious connection to universal spirit and supply will allow a pipeline of grace to come upon you. A thankful heart is highly conducive to faith, confident expectation, and living with joy. Know forgiveness in your heart, feel that the supreme loves you, and realize that you have forgiven all transgressions once and for all. With your forgiveness, you free your mind's mental and spiritual powers.

55. Being contemplative in action is the key. Having a focused and harmonious connection to the universal intelligence, while working effectively

toward your ideals, will continually reveal results. You are connected, a part of all possibility. Seize upon your divine rights to supply and success; allow yourself to be great and to do great things. There is no need to compete. *You must create.* Create new ways of doing things, provide quality service, create solutions, provide opportunity, and help others. Follow your true place and your dream, and your talents will be exposed. If you exercise the practical steps of gratitude, faith, visualization, and action, then the sixth sense will emerge, and you will know when to take action on ideas and fulfill them to completion.

56. Be patient and live harmoniously in a state of gratitude. The picturing of your ideals, coupled with action and faith, will lead to great things. Ask and you shall receive and be ready to receive what you desire. You may have challenges or even be dealt a blow of rejection; however, the universal mind allows for even bigger and better results. You may not get exactly what you want, but something better may be available for your receipt and cultivation. You will be protected from bad deals and afforded opportunities for even better ones.

# PART VI:

# THE METAPHYSICS OF BEING YOUR BEST: SPIRITUAL MANAGEMENT CONSULTING— MAINTAINING WEALTH

1. Responsibility is having the mental and spiritual faculty to respond to situations in a spiritual way with poise, courage, and mindfulness. The meaning of events in your life can be controlled. We should create the habit of attaching the most constructive interpretation to events in our lives and register the past in a way that allows us to grow and maintain high self-regard.
2. The totality of what we think and do is our character, our image, and our essence that is portrayed to all. Our character is a tangible energy that is radiated to the world.
3. When earnest desire is coupled with action, it becomes a living, faithful creation. Faith coupled with work IS being contemplative AND in action, which is the most powerful form of concentrated energy.
4. Belief is when you enter that mental state of knowingness and faith. For instance, we keep a simple faith in gravity and electricity and we believe in these simple laws. Therefore true faith, knowingness, and belief can force the universe and its creative powers to deliver a life force of

love, healing, and results. Remember, with all things created equal, faith power tends to move things in any direction of your belief.

5. Written goals are what freeze the snapshot of an idea in consciousness, and this embeds the code into your mind. Keeping mental blueprints nearby or visible is always an encouraging energy or force.

6. Planning is creating a mental design for the future; each plan encompasses many steps and tasks. With every goal are small and detailed actions that must be achieved efficiently and effectively. The tasks done successfully each day add up in a scientific way to augment your success quotient or momentum.

7. Persistence and dedication are the mental energy behind your actions. Staying focused on finishing or completing each task to the best of your ability creates effective outcomes.

8. When you have hope, it is the tiniest expression and seed of faith. Hope needs watering and cultivation; it must be brought up from a tiny sapling and nurtured with gratitude, love, action, hard work, and acceptance. Then it can become a real belief and an unshakable faith.

9. Many professional gurus and spiritual teachers stress the importance of personal development. We must continually learn, improve, and help others to help ourselves. This desire for growth keeps us honing our skills to continuously be our best.

10. Finding purpose is not easy for everyone. To force specificity in your life, write our things you want to do, itemizing them according to importance. Revisit the list on a daily or weekly basis. Expand, enhance, and build upon the list; remove items from the lists that are not productive or which may inhibit your

growth. Remember, the purpose of your goals is for your personal growth primarily but also for the benefit of those you love.

11. Outcomes are extremely important. Why would you do anything if you did not desire a constructive result? We all want beneficial outcomes with our relationships, health, education, financial security, and more. See your life results over the last three to five years. Write out a list of what has been excellent and then itemize what has not been acceptable. Analyze and review your track record. Do you want to repeat the last five years? Do you need change? What are you doing wrong? What are you doing right? What can you change within yourself to redirect your life into a greater journey that is more in tune with your natural purpose?

12. The totality of our actions, omissions, and thinking is what constitutes our character. Our character is what we are. If we want to experience a better world and better perception, then we must become in our mind what we want to be before we can experience it. Letting go of the old and allowing new ideas to evolve in our life experience is a continuous process. What are your ideals? Do you know what your ideal life would be like? Sometimes we must engage in contemplation to allow our natural desires to bubble up inside our hearts and mind. Change can involve letting go of old habits and mastering new practices; sometimes even a complete rebirth of our self and image is necessary. Commit now to constructive change and innovation.

13. As many top coaching professionals have said, finding your specialty is key. Become the expert at one thing. Master a specific field of knowledge and research. Be the best commentator at one particular

issue. You will become known for excellence if you engage singular purpose.

14. Sometimes we need to model or imitate the best to become the best. Find an expert in the field you want to enter. Train yourself to be like those whom you admire and respect. Ask leaders in the field what they did to become the best, and model yourself after that. Sometimes people create murals, picture boards, treasure maps, or collages that contain images of their ideal situations, hoped for relationships, or ideal bodily appearances.

15. Sometimes it is good to determine what you don't want in your life so that you can avoid such obstacles. We can all learn from the pain and failure of those who went before us. For example, we can see the resulting horror and suffering associated with crime, drugs, and ignorance. The rewards from being your best are priceless. Make the most of your time on this earth and be constructive.

16. To be in earnest and to sincerely commit to anything has great power, when you begin with the intention of having a successful experience. There is a supercharged energy that comes along with this commitment and focus. When you put the past behind and become determined to only look ahead, you eliminate much dead weight and free your spirit for growth. With a burning desire, your purpose is backed with persistence and enthusiasm; you will succeed and learn great lessons along with way. What is exciting is that your success may look different than originally expected but is greatly expanded from that original thought.

17. Struggling is *not* a requirement. As a matter of fact, life is quite exciting and interesting when we put the poverty mindset of struggle behind us. If we are

looking for struggle and hardship, we are sure to find it. However, if we see what we once thought was struggle as a challenge for growth, our perception can sometimes vaporize the pre-existing negativity. Each day is a gift. With gratitude and love, each day can include joy, awe, and happiness.

18. Generally it is our inner spiritual condition that drives our world view. If we can allow ourselves to embrace the goodness of the world, we can begin to expect each day to be new and good. After we make an effort with the strategies outlined herein, we will begin to expect good things to happen each day. We may even become determined to expect excellence in our life and in our mind, spirit, and health.

19. Let go of struggle, let go of hardcore realism, stop expecting the worst, and allow the inherent goodness of the universe to fill your heart and mind. Each day you have an opportunity to be your best and radiate love, tolerance, excellence, joy, acceptance, and kindness.

20. Remember that thought and feeling are the original causes that form corresponding conditions in your life. Thought and feeling are enhanced by self-analysis, prayer, meditation, visualization, affirmations, and contemplation.

21. Constructive thoughts, which are good for everyone, are more powerful than any negative emotion because the constructive thought contains inherent flow and harmlessness.

22. Making mental pictures for the exact purpose of developing imagination and focus expands the power to create in mind.

23. The harmonious relationship and unity with the whole of the supreme intelligence creates a

connection and flow of originating ideas to the seeker.

24. Ideal situations are the highest goals and wants that you may have. All thinking beings have a divine inspiration to survive, adapt, expand, and secure a greater life.

25. God is all intelligence, where each spiritual being has part of the supreme within them. See the Gospel/Bible (Luke 12:21) and the wisdom literature of Meister Eckhart,

26. Supreme intelligence, or God, is the source of the ever creative universe. Connecting to source through thoughts, gratitude, acceptance, praise, contemplation, prayer, and thanksgiving are the keys to forming unity. This practice is evident in the cuneiform texts of the wisdom literature of Sumer, which is the oldest civilization in the world.

27. Providence or supreme intelligence sends other spiritual beings to help us on our journey. These people can come from anywhere. Sometimes these helpers are referred to as angels, ancestors, prophets, or even the Christ.

# PART VII:

# SPECIAL EXERCISES AND JOURNAL WRITING

Here are some written exercises for growth and some suggested questions for you to try to answer. Be proud of yourself for reading and working these exercises.

1. If you could not fail, what would you do with your life in your work, financial life, or relationships?
2. Write down accomplishments where you have been successful. Begin with an award or certificate you received, or any job that you've done.
3. Write down who you think you are. Example: "I am a good parent, I am of Irish decent, I am a spiritual person."
4. Write down some ways in which you honor and respect yourself. Example: "I go to the gym and eat right."
5. Write down some ways that you may pamper yourself. Example: "Long bath, read books, play sports, quality time with loved ones."
6. Write down your ten favorite types of labor that you enjoy and consider fun. Example: "Working with people, travel-related jobs, creating things."
7. Write down ten things you could do that would dramatically improve your life. Keep this list open to addition and subtraction. Example: Read a Book or take a new training course.
8. Write down ten to twenty attributes about yourself, or things for which you are thankful. Keep this list open to addition.

9. Write down ten things that you like to do or would like to do to enjoy life more.

10. Take out your resume and update it. Don't be shy and add to your resume anything that you have done for yourself, the community, and your job; or any skills that you may have learned.

11. Write out a list of your creative ideas. What would you like to start, build, create, or solve?

12. Who are your favorite authors? Why? For example, did they inspire you?

13. Write out an appreciation list: name the people who have helped you in your life. Honor them with a blessing.

14. Write out things you like about yourself and your best qualities.

15. What can you do to become a better listener and communicator?

16. What can you do to obtain greater peace of mind? How can you limit resentments, anger, and conflict while also protecting yourself from any attack or abuse?

17. What can you do to become better prepared for life, success, and financial challenges? How do you build better self-respect?

18. How can you learn to discuss your dreams and plans with those who can support your ideas?

19. How can you be more attractive, more loving, more compassionate, and more helpful?

20. What calculated risks do you fear that would really benefit you and maybe your family? Example: "Going back to school."

21. What can you do to better develop a harmonious relationship with yourself, your own ego, your highest self, the universe, or God?

22. What can you do to better cultivate a thankful heart and a mind of more constructive thoughts?

23. What can you do to further develop your character and integrity?

24. If you could live or travel anywhere in the world, where would it be? Why? What would you do there?

25. Is there anyone in the world who really deserves a sincere apology from you? Why? Would it help? Ask a close friend, mentor, or spiritual counselor before taking this step any further.

26. Is there anyone in the world that you still resent? Could you pray for them once a day for ten days? Why or why not? If this guaranteed relief, would you be willing to try?

27. Are you willing to honestly discuss your faults, strengths, and hopes with another person? Why or why not? If this would help you grow into a better person, would you try?

28. In your labor of love, are you willing to give more than is required in service, value, and quality?

29. Are you willing to keep a written list of several things to do each day toward your dreams? Can you try to do a few things effectively each day toward your life goals?

## NOTES

✓ _____

✓ _____

✓ _____

✓ _____

✓ _____

✓ _____

✓ _____

✓ _____

# PART VIII:

# BEING YOUR BEST AND MAXIMIZING YOUR CHARACTER AND WORLDVIEW—THE PHILOSOPHY OF GREATNESS

We exist as an integral part of the universe, and we are intrinsically connected to the creative force of the world. Therefore, we all contain the same essential essence and vast potentiality of the abundant universe. Greatness is equally possible with each unique spirit and individual. Every person has a higher purpose to make the most of her talents and gifts. We can learn to use our existing abilities and latent spiritual powers. All of us can overcome challenges, heredity, and external circumstances by exercising the creative power of the soul. If we are to become our best, we must cultivate our highest ideas and ideals into our existence. Our spirit and soul is driven to bring the best into manifestation.

We must take control of our mind and spirit. We can learn to set aside our instincts for a higher order of being. To do so, we must develop a consciousness of spirit and a connectedness with the supreme intelligence. This is where the purest form of energy flows, and it is this force that separates us from the primal and the animal.

Set aside your pride, your anger, and your envy; rise above laziness, greed, and adolescent lust. Take control of your energies and your inner powers. These powers are your character, they are your charisma, and they create your aura of how others perceive you. The seeker of spiritual abundance must repudiate and transcend every course of action that is not in accordance with our highest constructive ideals.

Then, the aspirant must strive to attain the most productive worldview, recognizing that God is all and in all. We must come to believe that the world is not "all wrong" and that our thinking must be adjusted to perceive what is good, wholesome, and right. Otherwise, we may become predisposed to a world view that can only be described as a twisted realism that demands examples of failure, catastrophe, and misery.

If your mental habits demand evidence of these pessimistic things, then the supreme intelligence will provide them for you. It takes real spiritual might to exercise our awareness to perceive all things as beautiful, creative, and good. We should see that there is a place for structure, order, nature, society, government, and even business; these things are serving humanity in their present stage and are advancing toward betterment. Remember to view your family and your neighbors as always improving, and bear in mind that the whole world of men and women are children of God who are each on their own journey.

We must develop knowingness that all is right with our world, that all is good with our worldview. Being at peace and removing the clutter enables a higher level of contemplation and action. Further, we become more in tune and at peace with the spirit of supreme intelligence. Recognizing as a fact that God is all source, we can affirm in this way: "The spirit of God is in all and through all. I surrender myself and my will over to the supreme for guidance and power. Because I am a child of the father, I am endowed with the abundance to reach my greatest potential."

If you desire any good thing, see it in your mind's eye as clearly as possible, and hold that thought-form progressively in your mind until it becomes definite. Decide what your future will look like and how it will serve you and yours, and imagine having all this joyously.

As for wellness, keep your mental focus on enjoying health. The source or God is perfect and has no illness, and because you are part of this great spirit, there is no illness or disease for you. All things created equally, you can stack the cosmic cards of health in your favor with faith and love.

As with many things, mold your thoughts of how you would appear in your highest form. Act and think in ways that are in agreement with that ideal future state. Be that thought, be that thing, and think in correlation with what you want. You should decide now that you shall make the most of yourself. You can serve the world in no better way than to become your best. Do it for yourself, do it for God, and do it for love of others.

Believe that you can make the most of life, and know that the world is full of opportunity for all. There is no lack; there is only abundance. Each day that goes by, the scientific world discovers new planets, new galaxies, new energy, and even new species. Creation is constant and unfailing.

Begin to take small, bold steps each day to be your best. Each action, each statement, and each function is part of who you are. When you do small things greatly, people will recognize this wonderful power. You will soon become known as someone who is trusted to do greater and greater things.

Be a good person in your work. Exude greatness in your home, your relationships, and in your spiritual life. Become a constructive beacon of strength, goodness, and creation. There is no need to brag or boast, because if you act in all small things with greatness, you will be perceived as great with character. With a spouse or family, you must integrate compassion, patience, humility, and kindness while doing things well, and you will continue to develop trust and loyalty. Your attitude of poise and power will be infectious.

Your first duty to God, to yourself, and to the world is to make of yourself as great a personality as you possibly can. You can render to God and humanity no greater service than to express and cultivate your talents to the highest. Great works will seek him out, and all men will delight to do him honor.

We must begin to think with certainty and creativity; and we must be sincere and honest in our thoughts. We must form a mental conception of ourselves at the highest, and hold this conception until it is our habitual thought-form of ourselves. With all peoples, we must make every act an expression of our ideals or highest good.

The person who reaches this higher viewpoint and systematically engages productive actions has already attained a degree of greatness. We will benefit from the consciousness of wealth that we generate in our thoughts, and we will not lack for any good thing. We will be given the ability to deal with any combination of conditions that may arise, and our growth and progress will be unshakable and rapid.

NOTES

✓ _____

✓ _____

✓ _____

✓ _____

✓ _____

✓ _____

✓ _____

✓ _____

# A Visualization and Meditation Exercise for Results

1. In a quiet spot, enter your relaxed state of mind and take a few deep breaths.
2. Relax each part of the body, one by one.
3. Close your eyes and imagine a snapshot of something that you really want to happen in your life.
4. Detail the final result of this desire with your five senses. View and See it, Smell it, Hear it, Taste it, and Touch it in your MIND.
5. Imagine the emotions that you would have when this dream or goal or result is reached. Feel the emotions of joy and thankfulness.
6. Harvest the mental essence of how having the result or thing will function in your life, serve you, and help all involved.
7. Believe that it has happened in your mind and allow yourself to imagine the ownership of this result mentally.
8. Pinpoint and focus on the completed final event of success. For example, "The foot race is completed," or "The check is in your bank account."
9. Experience love and grateful feelings when you recognize and realize your vision. Know and feel it as if it is fact.
10. Imagine the benefits for all involved.
11. Be willing to receive all of this good on a mental and spiritual level, which allows you to take actions toward creating and receiving the results.
12. Make sure you have created ways to capture the result. Example: You may not be able to become the highest paid pilot without a license.

13. Send this mental vision into the world with joy as a mental letter delivered to the Supreme Architect.
14. Respond to communication from others and ponder your intuition. Be willing to meet others halfway and to go the extra mile.
15. Allow your dreams to unfold on parallel lines. Example: You may want a successful business in offering one product or service, but the laws of attraction and excellence may allow you to sell many other things related to it.

# PART IX:

# USING AFFIRMATIONS

1. Affirmations are positive statements to improve faith and optimism. They are meant to be stated in the affirmative. Each affirmation can be written in an "As if" phrase in the present tense, using "I Am" or "I Will," if possible. There is no need to use the "I am not" style because negative reinforcement is not as effective as positive reinforcement.
2. Affirmations can be for health, success, peace, safety, relationships, or even supply in the form of money.
3. Affirmations can be said out loud or in silence. Some people love to do their affirmations in the mirror.
4. A prime example of a positive affirmation could be, "I am healthy, happy, successful, loved, and whole. I am part of the supreme intelligence, and the supreme only creates beauty and perfection."
5. You should have the idea of your desired purpose in back of your affirmations. As an example, a prosperity affirmation could say, "I will earn an extra five thousand dollars in the next four weeks by providing excellent service as a salesperson." Money is the object, but the service and excellence is the essence in back of the object or goal.
6. The above affirmation specifies some distinct creative work and cooperation related to your prosperity, and it is not a blind or hopeful demand to receive something for nothing. You can always

affirm mentally or out-loud for blessings and opportunities.

7. Overall, we should state our affirmations with confidence, love, harmony, gratitude, and faith. With this combination, the universe will gladly begin working to unfold opportunities for us.

8. As such, a clear thought or idea that is repeated again and again is almost certain to manifest in the future. If the thought is held strongly, with gratitude and feeling and in a creative way that does not harm others, your desire will come quickly as imagined— or something even better will unfold.

# Contemplations and Affirmations

## Prosperity

I am the essence of success. The universe is full of creation and expands every day. New opportunities and new ideas flow to me. I open my heart to that power and participate in the divine ideas that come to me every minute of the day. I allow peace and prosperity in my heart, mind, and soul. I know that I am blessed, and I am thankful for the gift of creation and life expression.

## Health

My body is a temple of creation; every organ in my body is nourished and revitalized each day. In time, my whole physical being is regenerated cell by cell. My mental ideal of myself is perfect. Because I am an offspring of perfect creation, I am

SPIRITUAL WEALTH MANAGEMENT

made uniquely wonderful through this authority. My body is a vessel of my spirit and soul, which allows me to exist and create in this world. I respect my body and accept the power and opportunity of life, living and wholeness.

## Attitude

My inner spiritual condition allows me to have a high viewpoint of the world. I see the world as a place of kindness, and I become open to receiving the blessings of goodness from others. I see the best in others and myself. I am worthy of success and a wonderful life.

## Love

I do all I can to maintain a consciousness of love in my mind. I forgive all those who have passed through my life. I want the best for everyone and hope that all can live in harmony, peace, love, and abundance. I meditate on the words of compassion, understanding, peace, humility, kindness, generosity, and selflessness.

## Gratitude

I am grateful to all those who have come before me. I am thankful to the supreme creative power for life, peace, health, and the ability to love. Gratitude and a thankful heart keep me connected to power. Gratitude allows me to have faith and the knowledge that I can exist in a higher order of being.

## Success

I am successful. I am worthy of prosperity, abundance, health, and happiness. Each day my life becomes better and better.

## *Abundant Thoughts on Scripture: Classic Laws of Prosperity*

To all of those who appreciate scripture and wisdom literature, these passages are here for your meditation and contemplation. These transformational teachings are keys to having an effective spiritual life that is full of growth and prosperity.

1. When I think of lack or limitation, I now think of the Teachings of **Laws of Abundance. John 10:10:** "I have come that they might have life, and that they might have it more abundantly."

2. When I worry about my worldview and the truth, I can reflect on the **Law of Thought. Matthew 6:22**: "The eye is the lamp of the body. If your **eye**s are good, your whole body will be full of light.

3. When I want to procrastinate or focus on the past, I can remember the **Law of Action** and take steps each day toward improving my body, mind, and spirit. **Luke 9:62:** "Jesus replied, 'No one who puts his hand to the plow and looks back is fit for service in the kingdom of God.'"

4. When I have annoying thoughts, I can consider the **Law of Love. Matthew 22:36, 39:** "Jesus replied: 'Love the Lord your God with all your heart and with all your soul and with all your mind.' This is the first and greatest commandment.... And the second is like it: 'Love your neighbor as yourself.' All the Law and the Prophets rely on these two commandments."

5. When I wonder about my capabilities and ability to serve, the **Law of Success** must be pondered. **John**

**14:12:** "The works that I do shall he do also; and greater works than these shall he do."

6. When I want to react or become overly attached to a situation, the **Law of Non Resistance** comes to mind. **Matthew 5:39:** "Resist not Evil."

7. When I wonder about the government and authority, I recall the **Law of Obedience. Mark 12:17:** "Give to Caesar what is Caesar's, and to God what is God's." I then realize that my spiritual life transcends politics.

8. When I am harboring anger or resentment, I try to observe the **Law of Forgiveness** and the freedom that I receive by giving forgiveness, praying for others, and allowing myself to be forgiven. **Luke 6:37**: "Do not judge, and you will not be judged. Do not condemn, and you will not be condemned. Forgive, and you will be forgiven."

9. When I wonder if things will improve, I must give credence to the **Law of Increase** and consider helping others and serving humanity. **Luke 6:38:** "Give, and it will be given to you. A good measure, pressed down, shaken together and running over, will be poured into your lap. For with the measure you use, it will be measured to you."

10. When I feel unworthy, I should observe the **Law of Receiving** and become open to receiving and having a blessed life. **Luke 16:12:** "And if you have not been trustworthy with someone else's property, who will give you property of your own?"

11. When I feel lazy or unmotivated, the **Law of Compensation** often comes to mind, and I try a little harder to plant seeds of excellence and effort into the world. **Galatians 6:7**: "For whatsoever a man soweth, that shall he also reap."

12. When I don't feel like preparing or becoming ready to embrace life, I sometimes consider the **Law of Preparedness. Matthew 22:14:** "For many are called, but few *are* chosen."

13. When I lose focus on the good and become distracted from my purpose, the **Laws of Attraction** are indeed worth respecting. **Matthew 6:21**: "For where your treasure is, there your heart will be also."

14. When I am afraid to take risks, ask for help, change or grow, the **Law of Supply** is sometimes the secret to my transformation. **Matthew 7:7**: "Ask and it will be given to you; seek and you will find; knock and the door will be opened to you.

**Taken as a whole: cultivating ideas and desires, doing your homework, asking for information and help, believing in possibility, taking action, maintaining enthusiasm, and expecting the best are all ingredients to an abundant life**

NOTES

✓ _____
✓ _____
✓ _____
✓ _____
✓ _____
✓ _____
✓ _____
✓ _____

# *Beatitudes: A Supplemental Analysis and Prosperity Interpretation*

The Beatitudes is the name given to the best-known and introductory portion of the Sermon on the Mount, in the Bible's Gospel of Matthew. Here are some insights into the highest meaning of each statement.

1. **The poor in spirit—theirs is the kingdom of heaven**

   This means that we should remain teachable and be willing to grow. Humility is understanding your right size, putting the source of good first, putting spirit before ego, and becoming who you are meant to be.

2. **Those who mourn will be comforted**

   This implies that we should turn our will toward the spirit. Understand your private emotions and transcend your instincts that may result in destructive thinking and action.

3. **The meek shall inherit the Earth**

   Forgive and receive forgiveness. Through self-analysis, meditation, or focused prayer and visualization, you can allow for the highest thoughts to enter your spiritual mind. Forgive yourself and allow for goodness to grow in your heart.

4. **Those who hunger will be filled**

   Remain hungry for insight and guidance; never give up. The mind when connected to spirit is a benefactor of the greatest of wisdom.

5. **The merciful will obtain mercy**

   Think and project love and gratitude. Radiate your good toward all, including those who may have hurt you in the past. It is key for you to rise above past hurts and become the best you can be, while also affording kind acts toward others that will help them grow.

6. **The Pure in Heart Will See God**
Our thinking, our actions, and our omissions are part of our mind and character. Keeping a mind directed toward the highest good will always expand your abundance and its flow toward you.

7. **The peacemakers will be the children of God**
Bring harmony and win-win relationships to all without facilitating injury toward yourself or to your family.

8. **The persecuted—theirs is the kingdom of heaven**
Experience and feel a catharsis, absolution, forgiveness, and wholeness. Your duty is to transcend your lower mental states into peace, love, abundance, and gratitude.

NOTES

✓ _____

✓ _____

✓ _____

✓ _____

✓ _____

✓ _____

✓ _____

✓ _____

# PART X:

# LAWS OF SUCCESS

## Key Metaphysical Laws and Philosophical Concepts

### The Law of Cooperation

We must learn to cooperate with Spirit. We, as students of metaphysics, realize that a harmonious relationship with our spiritual-self creates a relationship of peace and success. We must clear ourselves mentally to create room for harmony and peace that fills our souls with constructive spirit energy. Then we must develop a consciousness of cooperation, flow, and unity with spirit.

### The Law of Modeling

Our external environment and our spiritual and physical interactions are important. If we associate with like minds of spiritual nature who desire success, we can excel quickly. Many authors throughout history have promoted the earnest study of success. By seeking wisdom, we find insight and learn to be the best by learning from the best. Seek the company of those who are constructive. Project and act out the ideal image of yourself. Learn to reinvent yourself and grow toward your desired character. Avoid people who are destructive in their speech, mind, and actions. You should cultivate the most spiritual and healthy mental states. Engage life, stay active, and help others, and other people will help you in turn.

## The Law of Thought Energy

We think, therefore, we create. We are builders of thoughts and ideas; what you think is radiated outward. Your thoughts attract like thoughts. Through constructive thinking, focus, concentration, action, gratitude, thanksgiving, and praise, positive outcomes will be brought to you. Be very specific in your creative visualization and desires. You are a magnet for higher good if you nurture an attitude of harmony and abundance.

## The Law of Intention

The courage to think what you want and to take action toward your objectives is the ultimate power. This ability may allow you to see in your mind's eye what it is you want and will do. This type of visualization and mental planning prepares you for each day's actions and work. In the present moment, we must do all we can toward our objectives. We cannot change yesterday or do tomorrow's work; we must use our mind and actions toward today's tasks and mission.

## The Law of Love Energy

Love is the quality of thought and emotion that will propel us into peace of mind and great success. Love all there is. Think about the people that have been kind to you, the creation all around you, the good that happens, the inventions for the betterment of humanity, and the positive happenings around the world that occur every day. Learn to love all and love yourself, and then love will be attracted to you. Love is a form of gratitude, harmlessness, peace, kindness, and compassion. Thinking love and giving love will liberate you into the fourth dimension of thought. Think of how you have been blessed, protected, and guided throughout your life.

## The Law of Optimum Ideas and Opulence

Thoughts of the best, thoughts of health, thoughts of harmonious relationships, thoughts of peace, and thoughts of wealth will project into the world and mold your destiny. Health, beauty, confidence, and success are mostly a state of mind. For example, we have all seen an average-looking superstars be regarded as beautiful. Thus, how we think and carry ourselves most definitely affects how we are perceived and how we feel from day to day.

## The Law of Natural Expression

To engage in life and head toward our true purpose is fundamentally important. People who relegate themselves to something that they do not want to do for their lifetime are inhibiting their happiness and their potential service to humanity. The abundance of the world effectively provides for all of us in many ways. Each person must seek out what he or she wants from life, knowing that what is needed will be provided. Nobody is stopping us from following our dreams. We have the ability to consciously think and plan our future, and we have choices and an abundance of opportunity. Ask yourself what you want to be, who you want to be with, and how and where you want to live. Think about the possibilities, with the choices of jobs, careers, business ventures, and creative alternatives that you have presently and for the future. Imagine the real freedom that you have right now. Then, envision all of the great gifts and prospects that you have in your life.

## The Law of Spiritual Energy

We must learn the effective use of our spiritual and emotional energy. If we live in the past and dwell on wrongs in our life, then our energy is dissipated in favor of the ills of yesterday. Do not blame your past for anything. You are capable of all things new—your body and mind can be renewed altogether with continued metaphysical focus. If we use our thoughts and visualization toward our desired ideals and mix them with our constructive emotion, then we can move quickly toward what we want from life. Prolonged self-sabotage such as: resentment, anger, hatred, and self-loathing will indeed inhibit our growth and happiness. Transcending the past, asking for forgiveness, making amends when appropriate, engaging in character development & self-appraisal, and contemplating atonement can free your mind from self-tyranny.

## The Law of Creative Source

All things are possible with the source, which works in and through you. We are all parts of the infinite power, a power ever carrying us up to higher, finer grades of being. Good is on your side; God is your partner in life. Your faith power will be induced through your harmonious and thankful mindset and action. Never underestimate yourself, never speak with discouragement to others, and do not keep the habit of doubting opportunity and good.

In Christianity, the Lord had the power to command the elements and quiet the storm. Your spirit, as a part of the great whole, has in it the germ, and the same power is waiting for fruition within you. Christ revealed through the power of concentrated belief that he could turn that unseen element into the seen, and he could materialize abundance in the form of: health, loaves, and fish.

The word "impossible" has limits. Impossible is a typical response by others who may not know the potential of any situation. Thinking that dreams are unattainable is a common excuse to not do anything. Remember to ask yourself, why not do it or why not try?

## The Law of Regeneration

The body has many capabilities: it can grow, heal, renew, learn, and do great works. However, we must realize that rest and relaxation are vitally important to this growth and renewal. The body, or temple, is renewing itself daily with new cells and cleansing itself of the old. When we permit our body and soul to regenerate, it will do so quickly if we are maintaining spiritual harmony.

## The Law of Faith

There are rewards in having belief and a childlike faith. This expectant view regards all things as if they are possible; it provides a viable probability of success and happiness. Be open to an inflowing force of abundance. Allow yourself to change for the better, take action, and move forward toward your highest good. Remember that success is always a reasonable option through faith.

## The Law of Constructive Thought

Begin your day with taming your mind with spiritual and constructive thoughts. Feed your body, mind, and soul with the best food, information, and spiritual energy. Act, think, and be good to yourself and others; ask and petition from your higher power all that you want. Hope and pray for the best to happen to everyone. Bless, praise, and be thankful for all things good. Empower yourself and your spirit with love, gratitude, kindness, harmonious thinking, harmless action, and serenity. Your needs will be met by the universe as long as you do not resist the gifts of abundance.

## The Law of Positive Energy

A new mental energy level is possible. It is a simple adjustment to the way we use our thought. Try to *not* complain for a whole day. Try to stop blaming, and quit making excuses for not doing what you desire. Your thoughts and character can be reinvented—you can be reborn. Your mind and thinking can transcend into a new constructive awareness. It takes effort, but anyone can do it. We must be persistent. In life or business, we must press on in mind to achieve the successful results that we desire. Each day is a new opportunity to engage several successful tasks with your higher vibration.

## The Law of Focus

Energy should be directed and focused upon what you want to expand in your life. Negative focus can lead to frustration. Therefore, the concentration of your thoughts upon the best and being your best (in mind and action) can lead to a life of harmonious and effective living. Life will become easier as you are in flow and not resisting everything, and thus making an effective use of your decisions, time, and energy. Don't worry about what was; focus on what you want to become and how you can help others. Each day, engage in constructive tasks toward your dreams and building high character.

## The Law of Spiritual Economy

Economy has been addressed by the greats such as Ben Franklin, and it is documented in the ancient wisdom literature of early cultures. There must be a balance in efficiencies and effectiveness to create the right amount of effort and results. Make the best of your endeavors and constructively use your assets and talents; there is no need for haste or waste. You can be creative and successful without hurting anyone, you can help many.

## The Law of Integrity

Your integrity is part of your character. Character can be developed to provide the positive impression upon all those with whom you meet and interact: you do what you say you will do, and you do it right the first time. People will soon recognize that you follow through on your commitments and that you are a person of strength, honesty, power, and trust. Further, this habit of following through with your obligations to yourself and others will drive you to be a very successful person. Avoiding things that are not a constructive use of your time will benefit all persons, and you will not engage actions that do not improve life.

## The Law of Preparation and Planning

A plan or objective is fundamental to the clarification of your desire. A large majority of people are afraid to specify what they intend to do. Transcending this fear and taking bold action upon your plans and strategies allows for the growth and manifestation of your idea into a reality. Preparing for your goals is fundamental, so plan what you are going to do and be very specific. Outline the steps needed and drive toward the desired outcome. Be prepared for outcomes that are as good as or even better than you desire. Know what you will do and prepare for any circumstance of importance. Be ready to act, engage, communicate, contemplate, and receive your good.

## The Law of Empathy

The ability to put yourself in the shoes of another will allow you to develop an understanding of others. We do not always know what other people are thinking or experiencing; thus, we try to understand others' goals and challenges. Let your kindness and gentleness be known. Speak and act with confidence, strength, and grace, and do not react to the world. Respond to it with poise and treat others in the ways that you would want to be treated. Learn to communicate and receive opportunities by first understanding what others are saying.

## The Law of Sincerity

Honesty is interrelated to truth. There is the truth that others speak, but more important, there is the truth of what we perceive and analyze. When we operate on this earthly plane, we must try to view truth at the highest level. If you sincerely act and think in constructive ways, then vast opportunity will be attracted to you as your truth. Like attracts like. You need not seek power over others. Give others the impression of increase, and they will be attracted to your value, service, wisdom, and the quality of your living. Be earnest in your character.

## The Law of Harmonious Relationships

Be connected with all that is good. Keep a harmonious relationship with the world through various strategies. Using gratitude for any of your gifts on a daily basis can grow your expectation of good and faith. It is much easier to be connected when you have set aside or removed destructive thinking such as resentment, jealously, other blocks and barriers.

## The Law of Desire

Desires are good and excellent. Desires bring focus on enriching your life and following your true direction. Cultivating desires into reality is vital for change, innovation, and improvement. You would not have a desire unless it was possible, but follow through on ideas where you have a solid sphere of possibility. An earnest and heartfelt desire is energized and empowered for success.

## The Law of Self-Reliance

You are to become rich in life. Spiritual abundance is yours—it is your birthright. Your sixth sense becomes available to you through your connection to spiritual abundance and prosperity. You are connected and harmonized with the universe, and thus you are cooperating and co-creating with the world. You will become self-reliant because you are moving closer to your true place, which is utilizing your unique and creative abilities. Your true place is your right livelihood, your labor of love. Your career and efforts will be further harmonized to become a wealth of opportunity and abundance in your personal and working endeavors. Remain committed to your dreams and your true-self so that your given talents will unfold and multiply.

## The Law of Having

Mentally seeing and feeling the outcome or result as if you have it already is very important. It allows you to see the rewards, and it further facilitates feelings surrounding the outcome. Harvesting positive feelings about the outcome is very important to energize a desire, mission, visualization, and result. Have what you want in your mind and allow it to materialize.

## The Law of Vision and Mission

A vision is important in that you clarify the results of your long-term goals and your destination. A mission is important in that you can quantify and clarify the means that will be used to achieve the desired future outcome which is part of the path or journey.

## The Law of Visualization and Imagination

Mental visualization of your objectives holds great importance. Seeing what you intend to do as if it is reality is a powerful mental exercise, but it is vital to the codification and building of the objective so as to assist the manifestation of the result. Seeing exactly what you desire and intend causes you to specify your wants and desires. The stronger and longer you can hold your ideal in your mind's eye, the better.

## The Law of Efficiency

Pointing your mental faculties toward the individual actions required to achieve a task, project, or goal is what causes effectiveness — as long as your acts are efficient. Continuous and persistent thinking and action toward your work, goal, project, or desired outcome can funnel or intensify the energy in a specific direction. Completion and finalization of acts and tasks, one by one and in a successful manner, creates momentum toward an objective.

## The Law of Boldness

Boldness and action creates the spark which energizes an idea. Boldness is what may cause opportunity, serendipity of events and draw people to be attracted to you. Therefore, contemplation mixed with action is the optimal, blended solution.

## The Law of Cause and Effect

Like attracts like, and every action has a reaction. Types of actions and thoughts attract similar actions and thoughts. Kindness tends to bring kindness; respect tends to bring respect. Additionally, constructive thinking tends to bring constructive opportunities and events to the individual.

## The Law of Increase

All mankind tends to be attracted to those who can bring more life or enrichment. If an individual projects life and opportunity, then he or she will attract similar minds.

## The Law of Seeking Wisdom

Wisdom is the ability to think something over, discuss it with others, or seek out counsel from those who understand or know the subject well. Thus, the use of lessons learned and opinions of experts are a valid considerations in thinking and acting.

## The Law of Love, Forgiveness and Harmony

Cultivating love and forgiveness can dispel otherwise destructive thoughts. Great minds can look back on things they love or loved, and re-harness that emotion.

## The Law of Self-Regard

There is something very real in taking care of yourself and your affairs, and minding your own business. Your enhanced mind, body, soul, and financial affairs allow you to help those whom you love, and you can serve humanity in better ways. The greatest way to be of service to your loved ones is to make the best of yourself.

## The Law of Gratitude

A sincere, heartfelt gratitude for life and its gifts will allow the flow of good to you. Systematic recognition of people or things to be thankful for, along with gratitude, may facilitate an expectation of good and growth of inherent faith. Integrating this confident expectation with your aspirations creates great power.

## The Law of Response-Ability

Speaking of only positive things can attract opportunity and friends. Guarded speech can protect you from negative forces. Keeping your desires and goals close to you will keep the energy of the new ideas from becoming dissipated. Sharing your desires and goals with those who support, encourage, and assist you can be a constructive exercise and can help harvest constructive feedback.

## The Law of Creativity

Your creative power IS your wealth. This gift is pure and free. Your mind allows you to develop ideas. There is *no* limit to the value of ideas and creation. Less educated people believe that competition causes a limited supply. However, creativity always manifests abundance for all. As an example, an individual who creates a new cure to solve a health problem is not competing against the world but is helping it.

## The Law of Right Livelihood

Having a labor of love can cause effectiveness and efficiency through enthusiastic work. Doing something that you believe in, or selling a product that you have faith in, can make any job much easier or even fun. Having fun with work is a divine right.

## The Law of Blessing and Expansion

People seem to enjoy a greater state of well-being and success when they bless their relationship with the universe, bless their loved ones, bless their home, and give thanks for their health on a daily basis.

## Law of Detachment

When we become too attached or dependent on a potential result, we could limit ourselves from the gifts of the universe. It is good to expect the best, but it is also smart to allow for something better to unfold. Thus, trying to control a specific outcome without any flexibility can inhibit the universe from its creativity.

## Law of Receiving

Many people from around the world feel unworthy of abundance, not valuing themselves, their service, their talents, and work. It is very important to learn to feel worthy, unique, and deserving of good. Moreover, you should become mentally open to receiving all good things in life. People should be careful to create ways to receive the good into their lives from the universe and from others, such as accepting a compliment from another person.

## The Law of Like Minds

When you engage a mentality of abundance and harmonious spiritual thinking, your mind will expand and increase when radiating love, abundance, and health. Thus your powers of attraction will increase. The universe will send people to help you; it will be your job to select and allow them to assist you in a win-win relationship to expand your abundance where all can achieve a richer and fuller life through these ventures.

## The Law Resistance

Types of resistance that inhibit your abundance, health, and connection with the spirit are: resentment, jealousy, anger, judgment, criticism, hatred, greed, pride, and mental laziness. Other subtle resistance occurs when faced with change. It is better to adapt than to perish, while maintaining your unique qualities.

## The Law of Willingness

Willingness is the key to advancement. Be willing to take action, take a chance, or risk failure or embarrassment. Without willingness, you may never engage mental, spiritual, or physical action that leads to good. Willingness is a vital ingredient toward successful visualization, belief, action, planning, and success: "Am I willing to believe, to try, to engage? Can it be done? Why or why not?"

## The Law of Inventory

Holding onto old, counterproductive ideas and unneeded things can keep you from growth, spiritual flow, and expansion. You should take an inventory of mental ideas and material things. Eliminating the ideas, things, people, and actions that create inconvenience, frustration, clutter, and resentment will allow freedom and harmony in your life. When you prune the tree, it allows for new growth; when you clear out your mind, it creates space for more good.

## The Law of Causation

Root out the cause of your failures, your inconveniences, your frustration, and your mental or spiritual disabilities. If you have a problem, there may be a cause. If you injured yourself engaging in a specific activity, you may avoid this activity in the future, or you can better prepare for it next time. Otherwise, you may pay for this repeated action in the form of more pain and suffering. If you have a relationship that always seems to leave you in pain, then you may need to avoid this person if you are spiritually whole and the other person is not.

## The Law of Forgiveness and Karma

You may feel you have wronged many people. You may even feel guilty for past deeds or encounters. However, if you feel remorse and intend to act as a better person for now on, then you have made progress. In any event, your day-to-day action and character of goodness and kindness will build your positive energy where the world will protect you and serve you.

## The Law of Humility

Keep an open mind and keep faith in the universe. Put your spirit before ego. Meek is not weak—it is strong, confident, cooperative, and advantageous. Developing an honest appraisal of yourself can be healthy. You can always improve yourself, your credentials, your relationships, and your business. When somebody has hurt your feelings, said you are wrong, said no to you, or otherwise attacked you, it is best to analyze when possible and discuss the issue with another supportive person before retaliating.

## The Law of Purity

Peace allows growth and focus. Clarity and concentration are primary keys to serenity. Being able to operate on a plane with singleness of mind can allow you to achieve great things. A person who cannot focus and achieve one thing at a time may never cross the finish line with any dream, goal, or aspiration. Overall, if you allow resentment, frustration, hate of another, or fear to dominate your thoughts, then your effectiveness will be diminished. Hard work is required to keep you focused on bettering yourself. Overall, your freedom, vitality, and wholeness depend on your effectiveness.

## The Law of Balance

Enough emphasis cannot be put on the necessary balance between body, mind, and spirit. It sounds easy, but all people need to honor their bodies, improve their minds, and evolve their spiritual nature. Many organizations emphasize that when you are out of balance, you have placed too much energy and focus in only one area of your life. For example, you can overwork or exercise too much, and potentially harm your immune system or muscles.

## The Law of Visual Affirmation

If you cannot paint the mental picture as clearly as you want, then try to use the material world to enhance your mind. Cut out pictures from magazines or books of the ideal things you want, and put them into a collage or on poster board. Rip out images of the home you desire, people having fun, distant places that you want to visit, or the lifestyle and types of relationships that you desire. This action can help you amalgamate the images to imprint them on your subconscious mind. View them daily and place them in a prominent place. Overall, imagine having these attributes or things in your quiet time. Sense the joy of living your dreams.

## The Law of Atonement and At-One-Ment

For thousands of years, mystical and spiritual organizations have encouraged self-analysis, confession, atonement, and even restitution. This spiritual house-cleaning can free the mind from guilt, shame, and even self-defeating thoughts. Forgiveness of others and the forgiveness of self is a very important process for self actualization and personal effectiveness.

## The Law of Pruning

The continuous development of character means letting go of habits that are not working for you anymore. When you prune the tree of dead branches, you make room for new growth

## The Law of Peace of Mind

Peace of mind transcends all material desires. Most philosophers define happiness as peace of mind. As we know, each of us has our own subjective version of what peace of mind would be; however, this peace would of course imply faith and a freedom from pain, ignorance, worry, mental misery, and self-destructive thoughts. Further, peace of mind is obtained by self-actualization.

## The Law of Opulence

Wealth and opulence are keenly tied to worthiness. Sometimes our minds are too wrapped up in hoarding and not circulating our abundance. Thus, it is sometimes good to simply act as if you were rich, and play the part. At other times, it is best to treat yourself to something that you deserve, such as a vacation, new car, massage, hobby enhancement, clothes, ideal home, or tools for effective work. When you begin to respect yourself in a greater fashion, your body responds—and the world also responds.

## The Law of Power

Mental strength is something earned. It takes willingness and effort to obtain potency. When we intentionally grow our latent powers, we are able to meet opportunities or challenges with preparedness.

## The Law of Courage

Courage is better than cowardice. Examples of courage are acting with boldness to help others, or even stepping up to your responsibilities. In today's world, perseverance implies taking action and not procrastinating. Without action, an idea cannot begin initial movement or obtain energy that it needs to manifest.

## The Law of Affirmations and Meditations

It can be argued that many people are best served by learning to become silent and open to the universe. I believe that that there are two types of affirmative personalities. One personality is best served with quiet communion with their higher self. The other is best served with affirmations and prayers that assist in changing their thoughts. As you can see, one is active and the other is passive. A combination of both would be excellent, but many people focus on one system at a time.

## The Law of Seeking

Life is growth and is a series of changes. Being prepared for change is the key to peaceful transition. We should keep seeking life, spirit and growth.

## The Law of Natural Expression

When you reach periods in your life that you are truly happy, it is probably because you are expressing yourself naturally on a level of spirit, relationships, creation, and livelihood.

## The Law of Infinite Growth

The world is overflowing with supply. As an example, the birds of the world can adapt, migrate, grow and provide for themselves. There is a never-ending quantity of material and substance to create what is needed on this earth. If something ever becomes scarce, a more efficient substitute is prepared or invented. Ideas, creativity, and imagination have solved millions of challenges in just our lifetime alone. The universe is in a constant state of building, innovating, expanding and creating.

## The Law of Change

Getting out of your comfort zone and taking some small action in the direction of your needs, wants, or desires can sometimes be the spark of creation. This spark can sometimes create a whirlwind of activities, insights, ideas, and help from others.

## The Law of Magnetism

As for charismatic energy, the great American author Napoleon Hill implies that we all have many forms of inner energy, which includes our forces of magnetism and attraction, or sexual energy. Hill's years of research of the most successful and richest persons revealed this astounding secret. Thus, concentration is critical to focus all forms of your inner energy toward your goals, influence, leadership, and desires. If you are focusing your primary energies in scattered areas, you are in essence distracted and diffusing your power. To prevent distraction, a practitioner must be able to transmute and direct all of their mental, spiritual, physical, and charismatic energy.

## The Law of Vibration

Feeling grateful and focusing on thankfulness will invariably change your thinking, your vibration, and how you react to life. It will also charge your spirit with hope & the expectation of faith and opportunities.

## The Law of Living in the Now

We must not live in the past or future. Sooner or later, we must learn when to work, and when to enjoy life in its purest form. Find out what you love to do, master yourself, and learn to both live and relax.

## The Law of Honor

What is honor? Being honorable involves your thought, words, and deeds. An honorable person is a person of belief, service, and charity whose self-control transcends all drama and hostility.

## The Laws of Self-Reliance

Freedom is better than servitude. We must learn to break free of overdependence or being tied down to anything that can cause injury over the long term. We must make the best of ourselves from a standpoint of mind, education, health, body, spirit, and harmony. We become free to express ourselves naturally and effectively. Further, it is better not to interfere with others in their natural hunger to learn, grow, earn, succeed, and work.

**The Law of Hospitality and Kinship** are better than alienation. Hospitality is a word that implies helping our brothers and sisters. What is key to the concept of hospitality is loving our neighbors. By helping those who want to help themselves and by being of service to those who can't, we open the door for the universe to shower us with continued opportunity and gifts.

## The Law of Appearance

What is the truth? Do we know the facts? Should we try to learn more? Do we have time to investigate? Do we need to take action? Is the meaning that we have attached to the truth or constructive or simply based on ego or delusional mind?

## The Law of Vigor

Industriousness is better than lifelessness. As we know, doing two or three things per day effectively can create massive progress during a lifetime. If we can help ourselves and help others, our family and community also benefits and excels.

## The Law of Giving and Tithing

Taking time to give money, service, or goods to divine recipients will create untold flow in your life. Life requires circulation of your ideas, your things, and your service, It is virtually guaranteed that your existence will be blessed and protected through your giving of yourself. You are not doing this to take advantage of the law—you do this to expand your spiritual way of life, keep the flow, and give back. Expecting something in return is not needed, because the universe will provide opportunity for you by your embracing this process.

## The Law of Fidelity

Principles are better than universalism. Being true to yourself and following your dreams leads to your happiness. We are all unique. We must make decisions, take positions, and take action. Sometimes we must chose sides. With that being said, we must be strategic with our decisions while also trying to intelligently foresee the consequences of each of our individual decisions. Those who are open to suggestion and seek to better themselves in order to become self-reliant and productive should be assisted.

## Conclusion

We can perform tasks effectively and efficiently toward our ideals, objectives, and goals. We must see in mind or imagination the thing we desire in its completed form: the system or method organized and in working order; the movement or undertaking advancing and ever growing stronger, constructive, and more profitable. To spend time in looking back and reliving past troubles or obstacles is to spend time manufacturing mental obstacles to put in your own way. There is no need to speak or think of the past; the past has taught us valuable lessons. We may not have achieved what we wanted or have been treated unfairly, however we have learned lessons and need never to participate in destructive engagements again. We must take risks, but our new endeavors will be calculated because we will be prepared for anything that comes our way. We can avoid certain negative events such as arguments with family members and engage healthy ones such as helping others or working on improving ourselves

All experiences are valuable for the wisdom they bring or suggest. But when you have once gained wisdom and knowledge from any experience, there is little profit in repeating it, especially if it has been unpleasant.

Our thought is the unseen magnet, ever attracting its correspondence in things seen and tangible. As we realize this more and more clearly, we shall become careful to keep our minds set in the right direction on self-improvement. It is our divine right to have a rich and full life with spiritual abundance. The universe will send people to help us and guide us. We will accept their help and create win-win relationships where all will benefit. Your spiritual and material lives should be vitally important to you for reasons of balance and also for personal effectiveness. What you make important to you will grow. If you make your family, your success, and your wealth important, then all will grow in your life. When you blend your visionary mind, your emotion, your thoughts, and your action toward what you want, you will indeed meet your goals and dreams, particularly if you maintain a harmonious and grateful relationship with your higher power.

Continue to make prayers and petitions. See in your mind's eye what you truly want, and do not be afraid to ask for anything that is good for you and for all. Hold that picture of your completed successes in your mind, projecting it on the picture screen of your mind with sharp and defined clarity. Claim it as yours and thank your higher power for providing it to you. Be grateful, affirm your blessings, and take action toward what you want. Send it out of your mind into the world with thanks and confident expectation, knowing that the thing you hope for or something better will come into your world and unfold into your life's path at the right time.

On a more practical level, life and many of the objectives that we will want to achieve will involve a fundamental process. This methodology will usually include an investigation, diagnosis, analysis, benchmarking, planning, action, implementation, monitoring, and continuous improvement. In urgent situations, we will call upon all of what we know to do our best in any emergency, but with most long-term goals, we will have time to prepare.

## *Concluding Exercise*

Take some deep breaths. Breathe in life energy and allow the old energy out with your exhale. Your mental state and vibration is important. Next, take time to energize the way you feel about your result or goal; think about a higher ideal that you want. Feel the joy of seeing your desired result—sense it and emotionalize it. Whether it be: [health, wealth, relationships, or success], observe your desired result in your mind's eye. Think as if it is yours. Think grateful thoughts for the imagined improvements or something better being manifested in your life. Send the wonderful thought out and into the universe with heartfelt gratitude. Take a deep breath and exhale, knowing that peace, health, and prosperity are your birthright and your reality.

# The Wealth Manifestation Process Summary

1. **Balance.** What do you want most? Balance includes health, peace, wealth, freedom, independence, and the ability to respond to life. For any project to be a success, the person behind it must be healthy on spiritual, mental, and physical levels.
2. **Growth and Adaptation.** Each of us has talents and a purpose. A desire or objective that already has our interest and enthusiasm will be much more achievable. Our natural expression is where we exist on a level of challenge, comfort, and excellence. Sometimes grace enters our life when we surrender to the possibility of change and innovation and move toward our true place.
3. **Action Abundance.** Do you feel there is something better? Are you willing to take action and take responsibility for your life, today and in the future? Is your spirit calling to you to make advancement toward your joyous purpose?
4. **Writing.** Do you write out what you want? Do you take time out each week or month to quietly plan or meditate over your ideals, goals, purpose, or objectives?
5. **Purpose and Specificity.** Each of us needs to clarify our desires, ideals, and thoughts. When is

the last time you were really specific? When is the last time you asked another person for what you wanted and were willing to earn it? When was the last time that you articulated yourself to others in such a way that your passion and heart was in back of your clear and unequivocal desires?

6. **Intention.** Have you committed and made a request for something that you really want? What is the reason behind your desire? How will it serve humanity? How will you use the result? Are your commitments energized? Combining your emotions and purpose creates an optimal force for manifesting.

7. **Goals and Ambition.** How would you define your ideal lifestyle? Most people never sit down by themselves or with their family to determine exactly what they would like to do. Each person's goals or peace of mind may be different and subjective. However, if we can spend some time to write out things that interest us, it always helps clear a path for greater focus, direction, or inspiration.

8. **Blocks.** What is blocking you? Have you taken responsibility for your life and choices? Transcend your excuses. Have you cleared away your mental debris of resentments or unnecessary fears? Example: Discussing and getting closure on past problems, or getting past the word "no" and asking for help.

9. **Meditate.** Can you see or visualize improvement, adaptation, and manifestation in your mind's eye? Can you project upon your own mental picture screen the things you want in life? Can you project what you want in color, with sound, with detail, and even satisfying emotion?

10. **Creativity.** Do you have many ideas? Do you follow your dreams? Do you finish things? When do your creative ideas come to you? Can you induce creativity or intuition.

11. **Fear.** Sometimes getting past the possibility of failure can be overcome by planning for success and even considering the worst that could happen so that you may have a contingency plan.

12. **Protect Energy.** Keep your ideas to yourself and only discuss with experts and those who have supporting attitudes.

13. **Livelihood.** What makes you feel alive? What gives you joy? Can you associate your aliveness and joy toward your true place in life? Remember, there are a multitude of occupations that involve the creation things that help others.

14. **Contemplation.** Can you make affirmations, prayers, or petitions? Are you willing to think or speak to yourself about what you want from life? Why is "I am" important? When you say, "I am healthy, whole, complete, and perfect," this means that the God in you is also perfect. The knowingness of this proclamation is very important.

15. **Blueprint.** The conscious and subconscious are connected; what we continually feed our conscious can influence our deeper ideas and beliefs. There are strategies to training your beliefs, and mapping and affirming are just some of these tools.

16. **Mindful.** Spirit-backed concentration causes co-creation—that is, burning desire.

17. **Belief.** Conviction with flexibility allows the universe to provide the best for you.

18. **Action.** Each task is part of a final result. Each action is a nucleus or beginning to bring a plan to completion. We must take action in increments.

We can compartmentalize our action and faith into each day. Some say focus on the now, and others say there are twenty-four hours in a day. Either way, using your plan to move step by step brings great power toward meeting your goals. We can also meditate or contemplate on completing each piece of the plan to move the plan forward.

19. **Tuned In.** Becoming open to cooperation and harmony can clear away the mental clutter so that you can have proper thoughts, prayers, meditation, and atonement. Getting harmoniously connected to the Creative Source.

20. **Effort and Allowing.** Many of us have experienced a situation where we resist a decision or process. There are ways to gather the facts, analyze a situation, see insight, and take action. Sometimes we can alter our mental state and become more in tune with flowing instead of fighting. Floating down a river provides a view, saves energy, and is the way of least resistance.

21. **Agents of the Universe.** Other people from the world are sent to help us. When we are in tune with a higher purpose while having inner peace, our worldview and energy will attract people from around the world to help us. It is our duty to decide whether to engage them or meet them halfway.

22. **Compensation.** How will your dream help others? What good does it create for others. What is the value of it to all people?

23. **Thanksgiving.** Whatever we bless, we expand in our life. Whatever we are thankful for will also pour more freely into our world. Mental gratefulness also can augment our perception from scarce possibilities into a faith with unlimited opportunity.

24. **Habits and Patterns.** If you have bad habits that are holding you back, you may already know what they are. Just thinking about the possibility of change is an improvement. Thinking about what it would be like without the bad habit, and with positive and freedom related to self-respecting thoughts, is a powerful exercise. This thinking creates constructive consciousness.

25. **Circulation.** It is best to give away things that you do not use anymore. Eliminate the clutter and donate old items to family or charity. Give a portion of your earnings to organizations that provide spiritual support for you or others that you love. Make room in your life for new things and advancement.

26. **Worthiness.** You are precious, and so are your creations, services, products, ideas, work, and efforts. Make sure that you hold out yourself and your services as valuable to all involved.

27. **Receiving.** How will you receive and use the blessings given to you? Make sure you have a method and plan to capture and utilize the good that is being sent to you. Take Action Today.

28. **Providence.** The closed mind is not open to new ideas, nor is it willing to comprehend new insights. Kind acts will clear the path for excellent things to happen to you.

29. **Continuous Expansion.** Become a better person, building character of self or of company. As Socrates implied, self-analysis is the key to knowing oneself; this applies to the person and to a team or organization.

The above steps are referred to as the Metaphysical Project Management (MPM) Process.

# Quotes on Prosperity and Abundance

- "It is wealth to be content." —Lao-Tzu

- "Wealth is not his that has it, but his who enjoys it." —Benjamin Franklin

- "Life is a field of unlimited possibilities." —Deepak Chopra

- "He who is plenteously provided for from within, needs but little from without." —Johann Wolfgang von Goethe

- "Take full account of the excellencies which you possess, and in gratitude remember how you would hanker after them, if you had them not." —Marcus Aurelius

- "Whenever anything negative happens to you, there is a deep lesson concealed within it, although you may not see it at the time." —Eckhart Tolle

- "If you want to change who you are, begin by changing the size of your dream. Even if you are broke, it does not cost you anything to dream of being rich. Many poor people are poor because they have given up on dreaming." —Robert Kiyosaki

- "Ideas are the beginning points of all fortunes." —Napoleon Hill

- "When you are grateful fear disappears and abundance appears." —Anthony Robbins

- "Everything in the universe has a purpose. Indeed, the invisible intelligence that flows through everything in a purposeful fashion is also flowing through you." —Dr. Wayne Dyer

- "Gratitude is an attitude that hooks us up to our source of supply. And the more grateful you are, the closer you become to your maker, to the architect of the universe, to the spiritual core of your being. It's a phenomenal lesson." —Bob Proctor

- "Living in Abundance and Prosperity is a Reasonable Option" —Magus Incognito

- "You have a divine right to abundance, and if you are anything less than a millionaire, you haven't had your fair share." —Stuart Wilde

- "Prosperity is not just having things. It is the consciousness that attracts the things. Prosperity is a way of living and thinking, and not just having money or things. Poverty is a way of living and thinking, and not just a lack of money or things." —Eric Butterworth

- "Most folks are about as happy as they make up their minds to be." —Abraham Lincoln

- *"And he shall be like a tree planted by the rivers of water, that bringeth forth his fruit in his season; his leaf also shall not wither; and whatsoever he doeth shall prosper."* (Psalm 1:3)

- "The Constitution only gives people the right to pursue happiness. You have to catch it yourself." —Benjamin Franklin

*Not what we have But what we enjoy, constitutes our abundance. ~ Epicurus*

- "Gratitude is the vital ingredient in the recipe for Faith" —Magus Incognito

- "We may divide thinkers into those who think for themselves and those who think through others. The latter are the rule and the former the exception. The first are original thinkers in a double sense, and egotists in the noblest meaning of the word." —Arthur Schopenhauer

- "The key to every man is his thought. Sturdy and defiant though he look he has a helm which he obeys, which is the idea after which all his facts are classified. He can only be reformed by showing him a new idea which commands his own." —Ralph Waldo Emerson

- "All truly wise thoughts have been thought already thousands of times; but to make them really ours we must think them over again honestly till they take root in our personal expression." — Johann Wolfgang von Goethe.

- "Great men are they who see that spirituality is stronger than any material force; that thoughts rule the world." —Ralph Waldo Emerson.

- "All that we are is a result of what we have thought." —Buddha

- "Wealth is the slave of a wise man. The master of a fool." —Seneca

- "Happiness is not in the mere possession of money; it lies in the joy of achievement, in the thrill of creative effort." —Franklin D Roosevelt

*Money is like manure. You have to spread it around or it smells. ~ J. Paul Getty*

- "Liberty is not a means to a higher political end. It is the highest political end." - Lord John Dalberg-Acton

- "We are what we repeatedly do. Excellence, then, is not an act but a habit." —Aristotle

*Money is like love; it kills slowly and painfully the one who withholds it, and enlivens the other who turns it on his fellow man. ~ Kahlil Gibran*

*Empty pockets never held anyone back. Only empty heads and empty hearts can do that. ~ Norman Vincent Peale*

- "The thief cometh not, but for to steal, and to kill, and to destroy: I am come that they might have life, and that they might have it more abundantly." (John 10:10, KJV)

Prosperity is not without many fears and distastes, and adversity is not without comforts and hopes. ~Francis Bacon

- "It is health that is real wealth and not pieces of gold and silver." ~ Mahatma Gandhi

- "Desire is the starting point of all achievement, not a hope, not a wish, but a keen pulsating desire, which transcends everything. When your desires are strong enough you will appear to possess superhuman powers to achieve." ~ Napoleon Hill

- "Move out of your comfort zone. You can only grow if you are willing to feel awkward and uncomfortable when you try something new." ~ Brian Tracy

- "You can open your mind to prosperity when you realize the true definition of the word: You are prosperous to the degree you are experiencing peace, health and plenty in your world." ~ Catherine Ponder, Open Your Mind to Prosperity

- There is a science of getting rich and it is an exact science, like algebra or arithmetic. There are certain laws which govern the process of acquiring riches and once these laws are learned and obeyed by anyone, that person will get rich with mathematical certainty. ~ *Wallace D Wattles*

- Within you right now is the power to do things you never dreamed possible. This power becomes available to you just as soon as you can change your beliefs. ~ *Dr Maxwell Maltz*

MAY THIS BE YOUR GUIDE TO SPIRITUAL WEALTH. MAY YOU ATTAIN INNER PEACE, OUTER SUCCESS, AND THE POSSIBILITY OF THE BOUNDLESS UNIVERSAL POWERS OF

# SPIRITUAL ABUNDANCE

# ABOUT THE AUTHOR

**Professor George S. Mentz** is the first person in the United States to be multi-credentialed as a lawyer, MBA, qualified financial planner, certified financial consultant, and licensed financial planner. Professor Mentz has held faculty and professional positions with top business schools and Wall Street firms. Mentz holds a doctorate of jurisprudence, a JD in international law, and an MBA in international business and finance, along with an international law certification. He has organized wealth courses at the top banks in the world and at accredited law school programs. He is an award-winning author and professor, and he has won two national recognitions for teaching excellence. Mentz and his wealth programs have been featured in the *Wall Street Journal*, Investopedia, *The Hindu National*, El Norte Latin America, the *Financial Times*, Forbes, Black Enterprise, Reuters, AP, the *China Daily*, and the *Arab Times*. He has published over twenty books and has taught over two hundred law, business, and graduate-level courses around the world.

Professor Mentz is one for the first online professors in the United States to be credentialed to teach law and business. Furthermore, Mentz helped develop one of the most popular ethics and philosophy courses for a New York Stock Exchange–traded educational company, along with creating the first Graduate Wealth Management Program for an accredited US law school. Mentz was also the founder of the original *Tax and Estate Planning Law Review*. He has been elected to the advisory boards of the Global Finance Forum in Switzerland, the Royal Society of Fellows, and the World E-Commerce Forum in London. He holds a professorial faculty appointment at the Graduate LLM Law Program and has held faculty status with several business schools globally. His companies have established educational standards and alliances, and they have approved operations in over forty countries around the world. Professor Mentz has recently been awarded a National Faculty Award, a Distinguished Faculty Award, and a Meritorious Service Medal for Charitable Service, along with receiving a Team Faculty Award and honorary doctorates for his research and publications.

Mentz serves on the advisory board and standards boards of the India Institute for Finance and Management, the Arab Academy of Banking and Financial Sciences, the Chartered Economists Association, the Latin Capitulo para Financiero, and The International Association for Qualified Financial Planners. He still advises on a consultative status to the US government on trends in finance, investments, business, careers, and jobs, to assist others in finding gainful employment or advancing their careers. In his early career as a political scientist, he was a coalitions organizer in Washington, DC, advising and writing communications for a winning presidential campaign.

You can contact Dr. Mentz at his website, www.gmentz. com

# OTHER REFERENCES OR AUTHORS OF INTEREST

Allen, J. (1998). *As You Think.* Edited with an introduction by M. Allen. Novato, CA: New World Library.

Aurelius, M. (1964) Meditations, trans. M. Staniforth, London: Penguin.

The Bhagavad-Gita (1973) trans. J. Mascaró, London: Penguin World's Classics..

Behrend, G. (1927) *Your Invisible Power.* Montana: Kessinger Publishing.

Carnegie, D. (1994). *How to Win Friends and Influence People.* New York: Pocket Books.

Carlson, R. (2001). *Don't Sweat the Small Stuff About Money.* New York, USA: Hyperion.

Chopra, D. (1996). *The Seven Spiritual Laws of Success.* London: Bantam Press.

Collier, R. (1970). *Be Rich.* Oak Harbor, Washington: Robert Collier Publishing.

Coelho, P. (1999) The Alchemist, trans. Alan R Clarke, London: HarperCollins.

Covey, S. R. (1989). *The 7 Habits of Highly Effective People.* London: Simon & Schuster.

Dyer, W. (1993). *Real Magic: Creating Miracles in Everyday Life.* New York: HarperCollins.

Eker, T. H. (2005). *Secrets of the Millionaire Mind: Mastering the Inner Game of Wealth.* New York: HarperCollins Publishers.

Emerson, R.W. (1993) Self-Reliance, Dover Publications.

Gawain, Shakti (1979). *Creative Visualization.* New World Library, Mill Valley USA.

Bishop Bernard Jordan (2007). The Laws of Thinking: 20 Secrets to Using the Divine Power of Your Mind to Manifest Prosperity." (2007) *(9781401917968): Published by Hay House and Bishop E. Bernard Jordan: Books*

Hill, N. (1960). *Think and Grow Rich*. New York: Fawcett Crest.

His Holiness the Dalai Lama, with H. C. Cutler (1999). *The Art of Happiness: A Handbook for Living*. London: Hodder & Stroughton.

James, W. (1902). *The Varieties of Religious Experience*. Longman Publishing, London, UK.

Jeffers, S. (1991) Feel the Fear and Do It Anyway, London: Arrow Books.

Lao-Tzu's Tao Te Ching (2000) trans. T. Freke, introduction by M.

Palmer, London: Piatkus.

Maltz, M.. (1960). *Psycho-Cybernetics*. New York. Pocket Books.

Marden, O. S. (1997). *Pushing to the Front, or Success under Difficulties*, Vols. 1–2. Santa Fe, California: Sun Books.

Mentz, C. W. H. (2007). *Masters of the Secrets: And the Science of Getting Rich and Master Key System Expanded: Bestseller Version*. Bloomington, Indiana, United States: Xlibris Corp.

Mentz, C. W. H. (2006). *How to Master Abundance and Prosperity—The Master Key System Decoded*. Bloomington Indiana: Xlibris Pub.

Mentz, C. W. H. (2005). *The Science of Growing Rich*. Bloomington, Indiana: Xlibris Publishing.

Mentz, George S - *Other Books by Mentz*. http://www.lulu.com/gmentz

Mulford, P. (1908). *Thoughts Are Things: Essays Selected from the White Cross Library*. G. Bell and Sons, Ltd., LONDON, 1908.

Murphy, J. (1963). *The Power of Your Subconscious Mind*. New Jersey: Prentice Hall.

Peale, N.V. (1996) The Power of Positive Thinking, New York: Ballantine Books.

Ponder, C. (1962). *The Dynamic Laws of Prosperity.* Camarillo, California: DeVorss & Co.

Price, J. R. (1987). *The Abundance Book.* Carlsbad, California: Hay House.

Roman, S., Packer, D. R. (2008). Creating Money: *Attracting Abundance.* Tiburon, California: H. J. Kramer, Inc., published in a joint venture with New World Library.

Scovell Shinn, F. (1998) The Game of Life and How to Play It, Saffron

Walden: C.W. Daniel.

Seicho-no Iye (□□□□). Books by Dr. Masaharu Taniguchi.

Smiles, S. (2002). *Self-Help: With Illustrations of Character, Conduct, and Perseverance.* Oxford: Oxford University Press.

Thoreau, H.D. (1986) Walden and Civil Disobedience, introduction by

M. Meyer, New York: Penguin.

Tracy, B. (1993). *Maximum Achievement: Strategies and Skills That Will Unlock Your Hidden Powers to Succeed.* New York: Fireside.

Troward, T. (1904). *The Edinburgh Lectures on Mental Science.* DODD, MEAD & COMPANY: New York.

Wattles, W. D. (1976). *Financial Success through the Power of Thought: The Science of Getting Rich.* Rochester, Vermont: Destiny Books.

Wilkinson, B. (2000). *The Prayer of Jabez.* Colorado Springs, CO USA, OR: Multnamah Publishers.

# TOOLKITS

For other books by Dr. Mentz, go to www.selfhelpbook.org .

For a free guide by Dr. Mentz to wealth management and financial planning, go to www.managementconsultant.us.

To learn more about Dr. Mentz or join one of his networks, go to www.GeorgeMentz.com

**New Books by Counselor Mentz coming soon!**